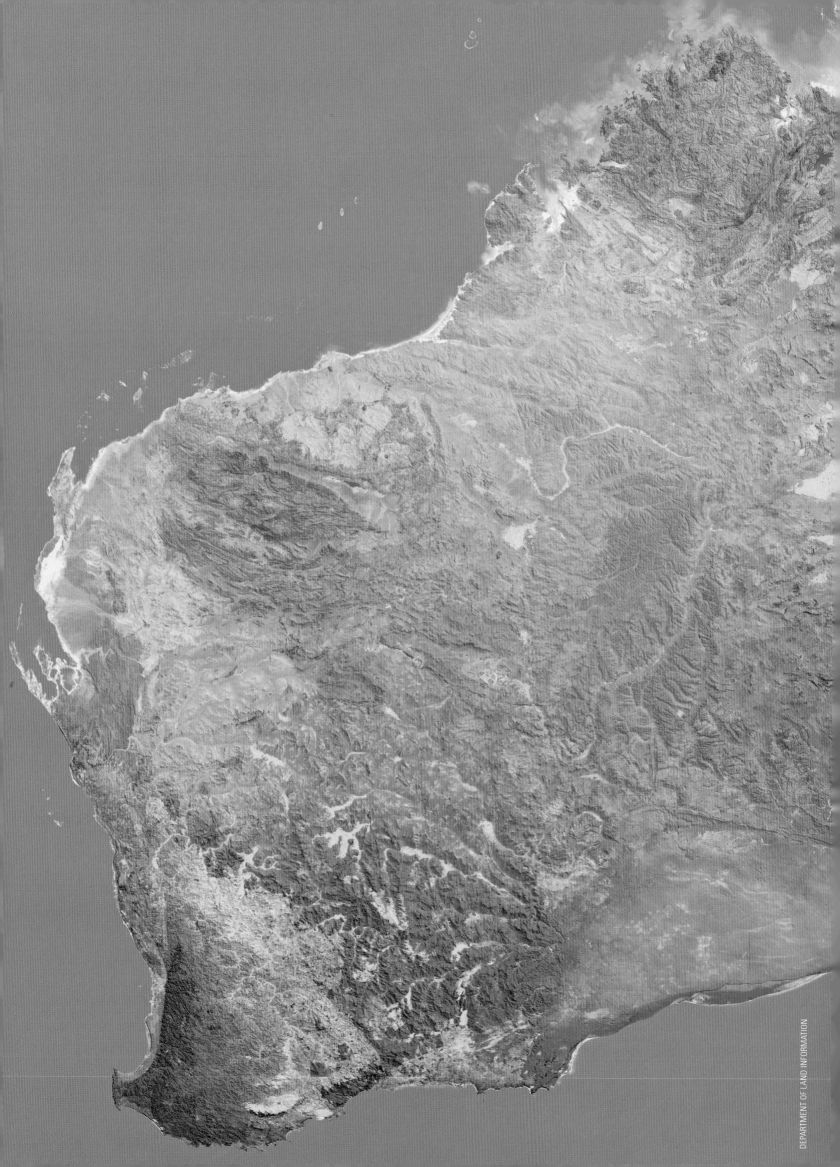

CHRISTIAN FLETCHER

Cover photo by Christian Fletcher. A canola field in Geraldton.
Opening page: A satellite image of Western Australia.
Previous spread: Camel ride on Cable Beach, Broome.
Left: The Old Swan Brewery on Mounts Bay Rd, Perth.
Opposite page: The Dingo Flour Mill is a prominent landmark in Fremantle.
Page 12: Sunset over Lake Argyle.
Closing page: The Joffre, Hancock, Weano and Red Gorges in the Pilbara.

ISBN 0-9758427-0-6

For bulk or single copy purchase information, please contact WA Business News on +618 9288 2100 or visit www.wabusinessnews.com.au

WA Business News
Level 1, 82 Beaufort Street
Perth, Western Australia 6000

PO Box 8352, Perth BC 6849 WA

Publisher: Harry Kleyn
Project publisher: Joe Zwiebel

Editor: David Prestipino

Art director: Marnee Rinaldi

Photographic editor: Tim van Bronswijk

Design and production: Marnee Rinaldi and Rob Leming

Profiles in excellence writers: Adrian Kwintowski, David Prestipino, Gab Knowles and Josh Bolto

Project researcher: Kirsty Bull

Printed in Singapore by Tien Wah Press (PTE) Limited.

GREG HOCKING

CHRISTIAN FLETCHER

Top: One of the vast dunes to be found in the D'Entrecasteaux National Park on the south-west coast. Bottom: Hancock Gorge in the Karajini National Park.

Opposite page: Aerial view over the Hamersley Station in the Pilbara. Top: Geikie Gorge on the Fitzroy River in the Kimberley. Middle: Relaxing in Handrail Pool, Karajini National Park. Bottom: The Stirling Ranges and a canola field in the state's south.

JON DAVISON

The Bungle Bungle range is a unique feature in the north-eastern Kimberley.

JON DAVISON

JON DAVISON

Left: Dinosaur footprints at Gantheaume Point near Broome. Right: One of the local inhabitants to be found in the outback.

STEF KING

MARCEL C DE JONG

TIM ACKER

Top: The stunning surrounds of the Pinnacle Desert in the Nambung National Park. Middle: Cape Leveque in the Kimberley, in WA's north. Bottom: The sun sets over the Great Sandy Desert.

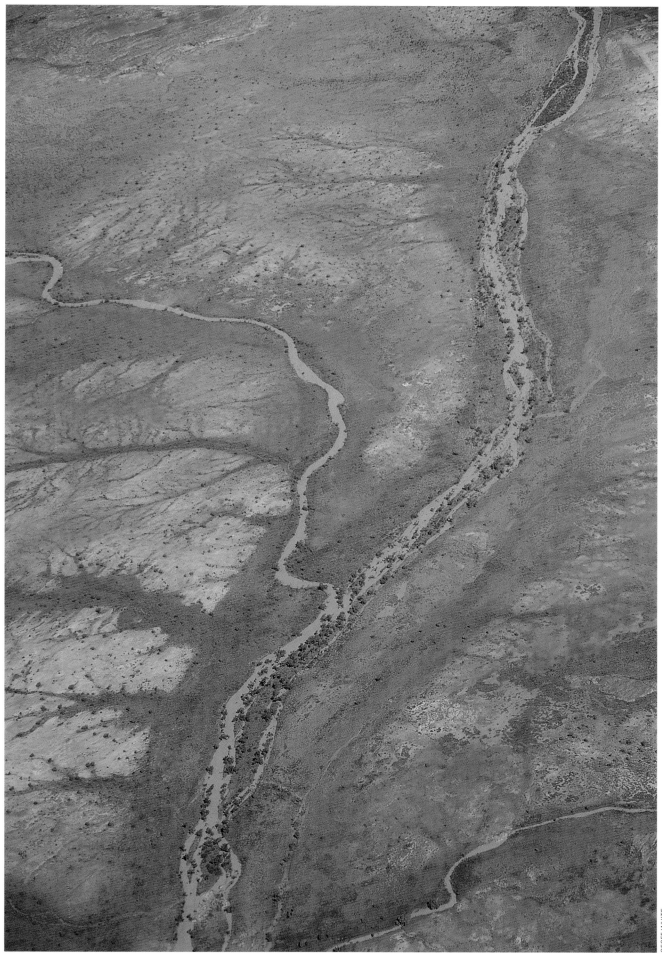

The river bed near Nullagine.

CHRISTIAN SPROGOE

The tailings dam at Pilbara Iron's 'Mesa - J' mine near Pannawonica.

Top: The rugged coastline near Kalbarri is one of the world's few remaining frontiers. Bottom: The treacherous reefs around the Abrolhos Islands west of Geraldton have claimed many ships including the Batavia in 1629.

GREG HOCKING

JON DAVISON

The sun rises over Nannup, in the state's south-west.

ALEX BOND

Thrombolites in Lake Clifton in the Yalgorup National Park.

GREG HOCKING

GREG HOCKING

RICHARD TONKIN

Top: The day breaks over Canal Rocks in Yallingup. Middle: Little Sugarloaf Rock at Cape Naturaliste. Bottom: Red Bluff on the Kalbarri coast.

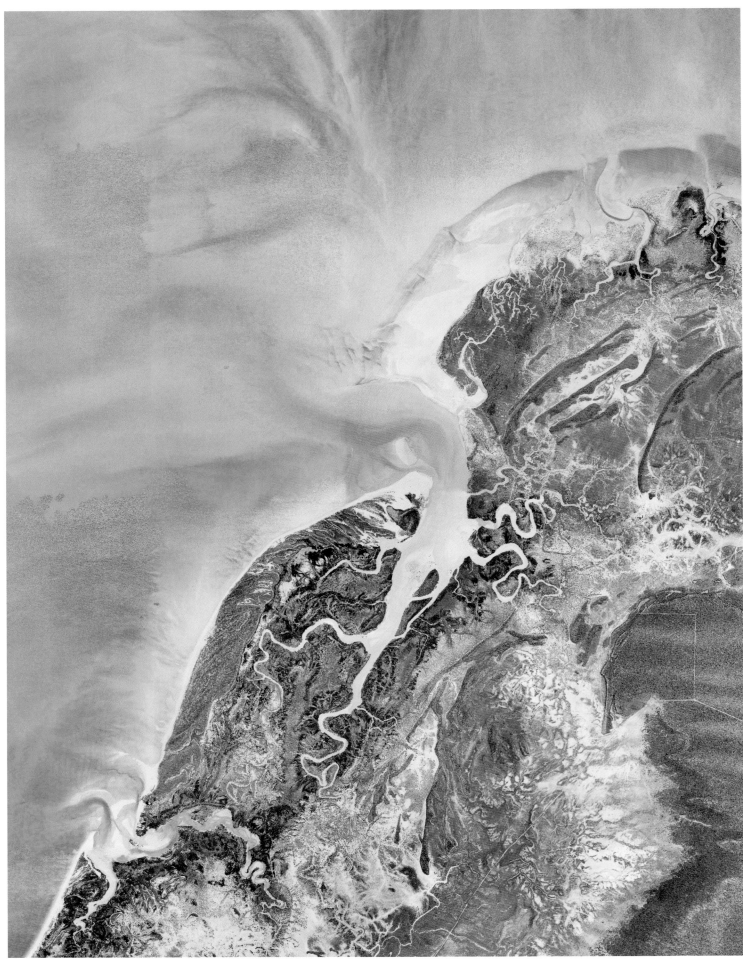

Bush Point, south of Broome.

Satellite image of smoke from bush fires in Pickering Brook drifting over WA.

CRAIG DOBSON

Waterfall in the Cockburn Ranges, Kimberley.

PAUL PARIN

PAUL PARIN

PAUL PARIN

Top left: Waterfall Tiers in the Karajini National Park. Top right: Spa Pool in the Karajini National Park. Bottom: Yampire Gorge Survival in the Karajini National Park.

DANE HAUKOHL

Joffre Falls in the Karajini National Park.

Top: A lightning strike creates an impressive display over the Busselton Jetty. Left: The Alinta Wind Farm, south of Geraldton. Right: A satellite image of Cyclone Monty over the WA coast.

KATHY SHERIDAN

STEF KING

Top: Footprints on Cable Beach in Broome. Bottom: Shells from a beach in Esperance.

Top: Anemone and anemone fish off the north-west coast. Left: Some of the diverse array of life under the Busselton Jetty. Right: This local wakes up to million-dollar views each day in the Cape Range National Park.

MATT GALLIGAN

MATT GALLIGAN

ALBERT GUNAWAN

MARCEL C DE JONG

RICK HORBURY

ANDREW DAVOLL

ZED RENGEL

Top: Eucalyptus Macrocarpa features an attractive foliage. Left: Acacia glaucoptera, or the Flat Wattle, is a WA native. Middle right: The Common Donkey Orchid. Bottom right: The Kangaroo Paw is Western Australia's floral emblem.

MORLAND SMITH

MORLAND SMITH

CHRISTIAN SPROGOE

Top: A herd of camels spotted on Great Central Road near Warburton. Bottom left: The numbat is Western Australia's animal emblem. Bottom right: A kangaroo and joey in bushland on the outskirts of Tom Price.

MORLAND SMITH

MARCEL C DE JONG

MARCEL C DE JONG

Top left: Cormorants enjoying the sunset at the Big Swamp Reserve in Bunbury. Top right: The south-west corner of WA is home to the Western Corella. Bottom: The Black Swan is Western Australia's bird emblem.

JENNY FLETCHER

CHRISTIAN FLETCHER

Top: Kangaroo Paw. Bottom: Fields of wildflowers present a beautiful natural carpet outside York.

MISTY NORMAN

DARRYL PERONI

Top right: A windmill deep in the south-west of WA. Bottom right: Making the most of farm life in Western Australia.

HELENA TAELOR

LYNN WEBB

Top: One of 50 life-size steel sculptures installed by British artist Antony Gormley on Lake Ballard, a salt lake north of Kalgoorlie. Bottom: The historic Hannans North Gold Mine in Kalgoorlie is now a major tourist attraction.

Top: The Exchange Hotel in Kalgoorlie. Bottom: An electrical storm over Kalgoorlie.

KAMIL SEDA

TOBIAS PORT

Top: River of Gold, Burnt Trees in a dry creek bed near Canning Dam. Bottom: A 360-degree panorama of Mundaring Weir, which supplies much of Perth's drinking water.

The Guildford Post Office was built in 1897.

JON DAVISON

Top: One of the many forests around Margaret River. Bottom: The Jewel Cave near Margaret River is a popular tourist attraction.

Above: The Valley of the Giants tree top walk in the Walpole-Nornalup National Park

FRANCES ANDRIJICH

FRANCES ANDRIJICH

Top: Picking grapes at Moss Wood Winery in Margaret River. Bottom: Keith Mugford checking the vines at Moss Wood.

Top: The annual Leeuwin Estate Concert in Margaret River features some of the world's biggest acts. Bottom left: Loading the crusher at Cullens Winery in Margaret River. Bottom right: The grapes are sorted prior to crushing at Cullens Winery.

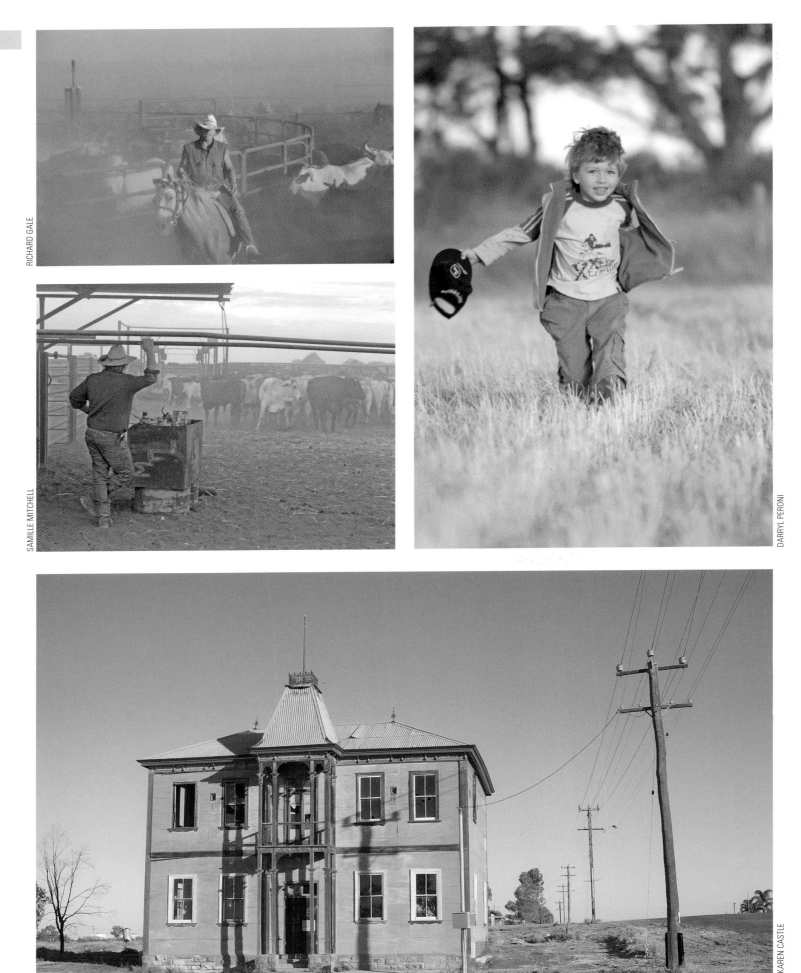

RICHARD GALE

SAMILLE MITCHELL

DARRYL PERONI

KAREN CASTLE

Top left: Cattle mustering off the Gibb River Road. Middle left: The Bidgemia Station in the Gascoyne is home to thousands of cattle. Top right: A boy runs through a harvested paddock. Bottom: The former Masonic Lodge in Cue.

Aboriginal Dogger Norman Ryan in the Gascoyne region.

HELENA TAELOR

HELENA TAELOR

RICHARD TONKIN

Top: In April 2002, 1527 utes, each with a dog in the back, assembled in Corrigin - a world record that has not been broken to this day. Middle: The West Kulin Woppa directs punters to the Kulin Bush Races. Bottom: A traditional outhouse in Cunderdin.

GARY BLINCO

RICHARD GALE

NEIL WALLACE

MICHAEL PELUSEY

Clockwise from top: The end of the road. The road to Nullagine. A traveller on the Gibb River Road in the Kimberley. Hector the prospector near Broad Arrow, north of Kalgoorlie.

MATTHEW GODDARD-JONES

JANE PELUSEY

Top: Father David practises the flute at the Benedictine Monastery in New Norcia. Bottom: Inside the Sacred Heart Church in Beagle Bay.

ANETA WNEK

MARCEL C DE JONG

Top: Broome's Sun Pictures opened in 1916 and is the world's oldest operating outdoor cinema. Bottom: A Boab Tree in Roebuck Bay, Broome.

JON DAVISON

JON DAVISON

Top: A water polo team in action at the Claremont pool. Bottom: Lawn bowls at the Bunbury Bowling Club.

Roadhouse on the Nullarbor Plain.

TONI WILKINSON / THE UWA PERTH INTERNATIONAL ARTS FESTIVAL

TONI WILKINSON / THE UWA PERTH INTERNATIONAL ARTS FESTIVAL

Top: 2006 UWA Perth International Arts Festival, Lotterywest Festival Overture, Welcome to Country presented in association with Yirra Yaakin Aboriginal Corporation. Bottom: 2006 UWA Perth International Arts Festival, Lotterywest Festival Overture, Unveiling of the Ngallak Koort Boodja Canvas (Our Heart Land Canvas) presented in association with Yirra Yaakin Aboriginal Corporation.

TIM ACKER

TOURISM WESTERN AUSTRALIA

Top: Aboriginal artists produce internationally acclaimed paintings at remote art centres in WA's outback Aboriginal communities. Bottom: Wandjina Aboriginal rock art, found in the West Kimberley.

CHRISTIAN FLETCHER

ROSS WALLACE

Top: The Old Mandurah Bridge south of Perth. Bottom: Fishing Boat Harbour in Fremantle.

Top: Sunrise over the Brcome port. Bottom: Sunset over the Exmouth marina.

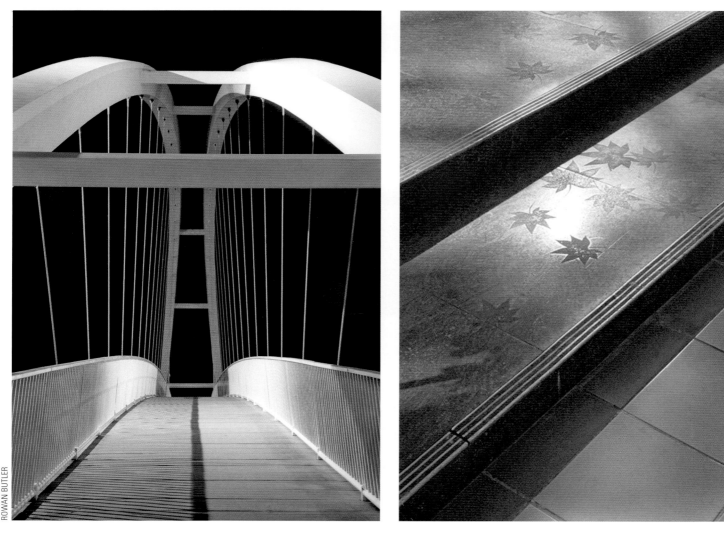

Top: Freeway overpass, Leederville. Bottom left: The Hutton Street footbridge over the Mitchell Freeway in Perth. Bottom right: Central Park steps in Perth.

Top: Sun sets over Lake Monger in Perth. Bottom: Kings Park's gum trees serve as a perfect backdrop to a colourful light display.

CHRISTIAN SPROGOE

GREG LEWIS

Top: The Swan River from Mosman Bay. Bottom: Fishing under the Narrows Bridge in Perth.

Top: The Busselton Jetty on a winter's evening. Bottom: Boats moored in the Mandurah Marina.

LUKE SIMON

JON DAVISON

KINGSLEY KLAU

Top: Cottesloe Beach looks inviting in the heat of summer. Bottom left: Soaking up the sun on a lazy summer's afternoon. Bottom right: Jumping in the waves at Warnbro Beach.

Top: Sun sets over Hamelin Bay in the state's south-west. Bottom: A novel use for a broken surfboard in Prevelly.

GREG LEWIS

BRENDAN HEAD

PAUL AMYES

LYNN WEBB

Top left: Skateboarder Renton Millar shows his skills at the Gravity Games. Top right: Beach volleyball is a popular sport on Scarborough Beach. Bottom left: Wake Boarding at the Gravity Games. Bottom right: Hang-gliding over the Great Australian Bight.

RICHARD TONKIN

HAE SOO SHIN

DEREK POOL

Top: Hot air balloons near Northam. Bottom left: The start of the annual City to Surf Fun Run in St Georges Terrace, Perth. Bottom right: The finish line in the popular Busselton Ironman Race.

Top: Surfers take a break at Rottnest Island. Bottom: Rottnest Island's iconic Bathurst Lighthouse.

Rottnest Island, just off the coast of Perth, is a popular holiday destination.

LUKE SIMON

JASMIN CASTILLO

ANDREW DAVOLL

Top: Smoke from a bushfire drifts across Ocean Beach in Denmark. Bottom left: Staffies and surfers at Mullaloo Beach. Bottom right: WA's beaches are not just about the sun and the fun.

JON DAVISON

CHRISTIAN FLETCHER

Top: Children at play in Thomson Bay on Rottnest Island. Bottom: Bicycles are the preferred mode of transport on Rottnest Island.

FRANCES ANDRIJICH

GLEN COWANS

Top: Even a man's best friend likes a dip in the ocean on a hot summer's day. Bottom: Snorkelling off the Cocos Keeling Islands.

LUKE SIMON

CHRISTIAN SPROGOE

Top: WA offers a great lifestyle. Bottom: Surfer at the 'Isolators', south of Cottesloe.

DANNY KHOO

Weddings are a joyous event for all involved.

STEF KING

ALBERT GUNAWAN

Top: A North Fremantle wedding. Bottom: A local wedding.

TONI WILKINSON / THE UWA PERTH INTERNATIONAL ARTS FESTIVAL

The 2004 UWA Perth International Arts Festival, Lotterywest Festival Finale, Cottesloe Beach.

ROEL LOOPERS

ROEL LOOPERS

BRENDAN HEAD

Top: The colourful Fremantle Festival parade. Middle: Fremantle's annual Blessing of the Fleet is steeped in tradition. Bottom: Belly dancing at the Subiaco Street Festival.

Top left: Fresh produce abounds at the Fremantle Markets. Top right: Sunday afternoon on South Terrace in Fremantle. Middle left: Accordion player entertains at the Subiaco Street Festival. Middle right: Alfresco dining is a great way to spend an evening with friends in Northbridge. Bottom: The Sail and Anchor Hotel in Fremantle.

Top: Boats moored on the Swan River. Bottom left: Sailing on the Swan River from the Royal Freshwater Bay Yacht Club. Bottom right: Sailing on the Indian Ocean off Fremantle.

TOURISM WESTERN AUSTRALIA

TOURISM WESTERN AUSTRALIA

TOURISM WESTERN AUSTRALIA

Top: Kakulas Brothers produce store in Northbridge. Middle: Old friends catch up for a coffee in Fremantle. Bottom: Relaxing on the cappuccino strip on South Terrace in Fremantle.

Top: Time out in Forrest Place, Perth. Bottom: Alex and Chickie.

DANNY KHOO

DANNY KHOO

SPRINKLER
STOP VALVE
INSIDE

DANNY KHOO

DANNY KHOO

Top right: A street performer entertains the crowd in the Murray Street Mall in Perth. Middle left: A busker with a feathered friend. Middle right: A street performer takes a well-earned break. Bottom right: Gino.

Brian's fruit stall in Perth.

MATTHEW GODDARD-JONES

MATTHEW GODDARD-JONES

MATTHEW GODDARD-JONES

Top: Ballroom dancing competition at The Embassy Ballroom in Carlisle. Bottom left: Surf Lifesavers at City Beach. Bottom right: Competitors are ready to go in the annual Rottnest Channel Swim from Cottesloe Beach to Thomson Bay.

MATTHEW GODDARD-JONES

MATTHEW GODDARD-JONES

Top: Cyclists on The Great Bike Hike. Bottom: Lawn Bowls Championship at the Floreat Bowling Club.

GARY BLINCO

HEATHER READING

HEATHER READING

Left: Anzac Pride. Top right: The Anzac Memorial on Monument Hill in Fremantle. Bottom right: The Anzac Day Parade in Perth.

LET SILENT CONTEMPLATION BE YOUR OFFERING

Top: The Flame of Remembrance burns in the Pool of Reflection at the State War Memorial in Kings Park. Bottom: Proud to be an Aussie.

TIM VAN BRONSWIJK

CALLUM PONTON

WENDY D'SOUZA

Clockwise from top: One of the rides at the Perth Royal Show. Bottom left: Laughing clowns at the Perth Royal Show. Bottom right: The Python Loop at the Perth Royal Show.

CALLUM PONTON

JON DAVISON

Top: Fireworks over Perth and the Swan River at the annual Australia Day Skyshow. Bottom: Matilda Bay on the Swan river is a perfect spot to watch the annual Australia Day Skyshow from.

MARCEL C DE JONG

JON DAVISON

JON DAVISON

Top: Autumn arrives at the University of Western Australia. Left: The sun setting through the trees and builings at the University of Western Australia. Right: The Royal Aero Club of WA's Werner Buhlmann in his restored Tiger Moth above Perth.

The Duyfken replica moored at the Old Swan Brewery on the Swan River in Perth.

TIM VAN BRONSWIJK

MARCEL C DE JONG

Top: The Perth Convention Exhibition Centre. Bottom: The Narrows Bridge stretches across the Swan River from the city to South Perth.

The Swan Bell Tower in Perth.

CRAIG HILTON

The Moores Building in Fremantle.

Top: The Fremantle Prison, built by convicts in the 1850s, housed inmates until 1991. It is now a fascinating tourist attraction. Middle: The Fremantle Port at dusk. Bottom: The WA Maritime Museum and the A-shed in the historic Fremantle Harbour.

JON DAVISON

The Collins Class Submarine HMAS Rankin leaves Garden Island, south of Perth. Western Australia is the home to Australia's submarine fleet.

Rigging the Leeuwin II.

104

KEN MATTS / HYUNDAI HOPMAN CUP

PERTH WILDCATS

PERTH ORIELS

TIM VAN BRONSWIJK

Top left: The Hopman Cup sees some of the world's top tennis players come to Perth. Top right: Perth Wildcats captain and Australian co-captain Tony Ronaldson is one of the stars of the NBL. Bottom left: Perth Oriels centre and Australian representative Jess Shynn in action. Bottom right: State cricket is played at the WACA Ground in East Perth.

TOURISM WESTERN AUSTRALIA

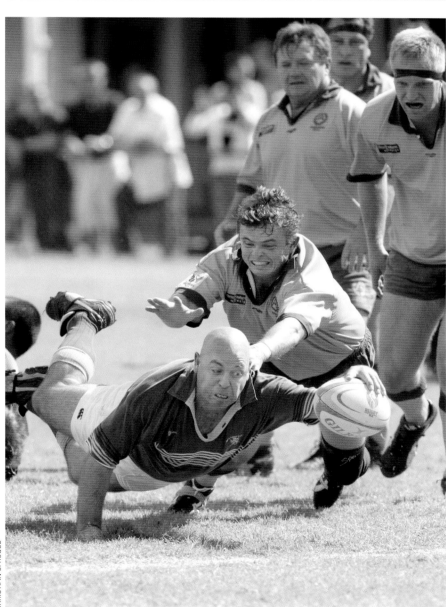

CHRISTIAN SPROGOE

CHRISTIAN SPROGOE

Top: Super 14 rugby kicked off in WA in February 2006 with the Western Force's first home match at Subiaco Oval. Bottom left: Nedlands' Mike Ryburn scores a try during the 2004 Rugby WA finals. Bottom right: Western Force player Digby Ioane runs through a tackle from George Gregan at Subiaco Oval in the Force's first home game.

CHRISTIAN SPROGOE

FREMANTLE FOOTBALL CLUB

RICHARD GILES

Top: Western Force fans getting in to the spirit at Subiaco Oval. Middle: Fremantle Dockers fans showing their support. Bottom: One Perth Glory supporter who isn't afraid to show his true colours.

JON DAVISON

FREMANTLE FOOTBALL CLUB

BILL CRABB / WEST COAST EAGLES FOOTBALL CLUB

CHRISTIAN SPROGOE

Top: Junior footballers from the West Coast Junior Football Club in action. Middle left: WA-born Matthew Carr shoots for goal in the local derby between the Fremantle Dockers and the West Coast Eagles. Middle right: West Coast Eagle Ashley Sampi breaks a tackle against the Western Bulldogs in the AFL. Bottom left: Perth Glory champion striker Bobby Despotovski in action.

Top: A power boat cuts through Extracts Weir during the Avon Descent. Middle left: Avon Descent paddlers at the Extracts Weir. Middle right: Paddlers in the Avon Descent - one of the world's premier white-water races. Bottom right: A surf ski navigates the Extracts Weir in the Avon Descent.

Top: Limbering up on Cottesloe Beach before the start of the Rottnest Channel Swim. Middle: Swimmers await the early morning start of the Busselton Ironman. Bottom: Sprinting to the finish line in the Busselton Ironman competition.

TIM VAN BRONSWIJK

DARRYL PERONI

PAUL AMYES

TIM VAN BRONSWIJK

Top left: Cycling at the Speed Dome in Midvale. Top right: Hanging on tight at the Boddington Rodeo. Middle left: Taking a jump at Rally Australia. Bottom: A Subaru World Rally Championship car during Perth's Rally Australia.

Top: Professional surfer Drew Everest catches a wave at Scarborough Beach. Bottom: Surfing on the sand dunes near Lancelin is a fun pastime.

TIM VAN BRONSWIJK

CHRISTIAN SPROGOE

Top: The South Fremantle Power Station closed in 1985 after 34 years of service. Bottom: Tho old boat shed on the Swan River, near Mounts Bay Road in Perth.

Taking a break before the dinner rush at Jackson's Restaurant in Highgate.

TIM VAN BRONSWIJK

TOURISM WESTERN AUSTRALIA

CHRISTIAN SPROGOE

Top: The State War Memorial in Kings Park overlooks some of Perth's tallest buildings. Bottom left: The Lotterywest Federation Walkway in Kings Park. Bottom right: The city skyline looks impressive from East Perth.

Top: His Majesty's Theatre opened on Christmas eve 1904 and has been entertaining crowds of theatre-goers ever since. Bottom: Arriving in style at His Majesty's Theatre in Perth.

CHRISTIAN SPROGOE

CHRISTIAN SPROGOE

CHRISTIAN SPROGOE

Top: Reclaiming Iron Ore stockpiles for ship loading at Cape Lambert near Wickham. Middle: A loaded iron ore train leaves Pilbara Iron's 'Mesa - J' site near Pannawonica, heading for the port in Cape Lambert. Bottom: Pilbara Iron's Mt Tom Price Processing Plant in Tom Price.

Top: The CBH grain loading facility in Kwinana, south of Perth. Bottom: Harvesting wheat near Ongerup.

JON DAVISON

KEVIN O'BRIEN

Top: A container ship comes into port in Fremantle. Bottom: Fishing boats moored in Exmouth Harbour await their next trip.

Top: The moon sets behind one of Apache Energy's offshore oil rigs near Varanus Island on the North-West Shelf. Bottom: Drilling for oil.

DARRYL PERONI

MATT GALLIGAN

Top: Herded sheep ready for shearing. Bottom: A shearing shed near Kojonup.

JON DAVISON

An outback sheep station near Geraldton.

CHRISTIAN SPROGOE

JON DAVISON

Top: Haul trucks at Pilbara Iron's West Angelas mine. Bottom: The Super Pit in Kalgoorlie is one of the world's biggest open cut gold mines.

Top: Esperance Port - the deepest port in southern Australia. Bottom: Ship loading at the Esperance Port.

124

MIKE WISHART

TIM VAN BRONSWIJK

CLAIRE HARWOOD

Top: The WA Maritime Museum at night. Bottom left: An architectual detail of the Perth Convention Exhibition Centre. Bottom right: The Swan Bell Tower in Perth.

Top left: Nickel refinery in Kwinana, south of Perth. Bottom left: A mine headframe in Kalgoorlie. Bottom right: One of Apache Energy's oil rigs near Varanus Island on the North-West Shelf.

FRANCES ANDRIJICH

Rows of vines in Margaret River.

Top: Rows of vines at Picardy Winery, Pemberton in the states south-west. Bottom: Hay Bales around Wilyabrup in the state's south-west.

JON DAVISON

JON DAVISON

Top: Winter burn off, Margaret River Bottom: Camping under the stars in Karajini National Park.

Star trails over Broome.

PROFILES IN EXCELLENCE

Richly endowed with natural resources, entrepreneurial vigour and a creative workforce, Western Australia's economy continues to grow.

The following profiles showcase the best of the state's enterprise. Each has a transcendant, and in some cases historic connection to Western Australia.

Whether government or nonprofit, professional service or cutting edge entrepreneurial, these organisations are integrally connected to the pulse of the region, and poised to contribute in vibrant ways to a future bright indeed.

1829 – 1974

YEAR EST.	COMPANY NAME	PAGE
1829	The City of Perth	132
1829	Lionel Samson & Son	134
1829	Plantagenet Wines	135
1829	Sadleirs Transport	136
1829	Sadleirs International	137
1857	The Swan Brewery	138
1897	Fremantle Ports	140
1898	City of Belmont	142
1920	Wray & Associates	144
1922	Jackson McDonald	146
1922	RSM Bird Cameron	148
1933	Lotterywest	150
1941	HBF	152
1944	Westralia Aiports Corporation – Perth Airport	154
1954	Woodside	156
1963	Skywest Airlines	162
1965	The Dowerin GWN Machinery Field Days	164
1969	Consolidated Minerals Ltd	166
1970	Mitsui Iron Ore Development	168
1974	BGC (Australia) Pty Ltd	170
1974	Marketforce	172

THE CITY OF PERTH

The City of Perth has tied together Perth's unparalleled natural environment, a thriving business centre and vibrant entertainment precinct to create a capital city that is the heart and soul of Western Australia.

Below: A black swan glides across the city skyline.

As the local government in charge of the state's capital, the City of Perth is well-known on the national and international stage. It has helped establish Perth as one of the most beautiful, and most liveable, cities in the world. Part of the attraction is its location on a broad expanse of the Swan River flanked by the bushland of Kings Park. The other, is its prosperous commerce and business district and lively entertainment areas.

The City of Perth had its origins in 1829 when the British government established the Swan River Colony, with Perth the main settlement. It formally attained 'City' status in 1856 and the council held its first meeting in 1858. The area has changed dramatically over the years from a pastoral and agricultural-based community into a 21st-century centre of commerce and business, with a strong mining and resources focus.

A Lord Mayor, eight councillors and about 500 employees run the financially sound local government authority, based in Council House, on St Georges Terrace. The approachable City balances the needs of more than 10,000 residents with a workforce population of 100,000, engaging with stakeholders through regular community forums.

The City of Perth is committed to providing a place of home, business, relaxation and entertainment for West Australians and visitors. It aims for Perth to be widely acclaimed as a city of regional and international significance, especially in the Asian region. The council believes the city's future economic development and "quality of life" are interdependent. The quality of the urban environment affects the city's ability to attract investment and generate wealth. With the increasing mobility of investment and people, a city's ability to provide a liveable and sustainable environment will be the point of comparison.

The inner city achieved greater focus when the City of Perth area was split into four different local government entities (City of Perth and the Towns of Vincent, Victoria Park and Cambridge) in 1994. Since then, the council has worked hard to create strong links between the CBD, Northbridge and new residential communities, such as East Perth.

Northbridge is renowned as Australia's premier nightlife precinct and a magnet for tourists and Perth residents alike. The City is committed to broadening the economic base of Northbridge while stimulating its creative industries. It hopes to achieve this by developing a piazza, or people hub, in the centre of Northbridge. Links between the CBD and the entertainment precinct will become more seamless as plans to sink the railway lines in Northbridge come to fruition.

Disused industrial land in East Perth has become home to one of the most progressive and imaginative up-market residential developments in Australia. The work was undertaken by the East Perth Redevelopment Authority but the City of Perth now manages the area.

This redevelopment is one example of Perth's business and residential growth creating new demands and expectations for the council.

Construction of the southern suburbs' railway and the establishment of the Perth Convention Exhibition Centre have spurred commercial and residential development in the western end of the city. Sending the railway underground has also had a significant impact and redevelopment of land in the city centre has led to an invigorated retail heart. The City of Perth has embarked on a major overhaul of the city's malls and principal public places. Hay Street Mall has been upgraded with a complete repaving, installation of new street furniture and plants, new lighting and improved security features. Similar upgrades will proceed in the Murray Street Mall, Forrest Place and the forecourt of Perth Railway Station.

The innovative City is also enhancing its open spaces and parks to make them more desirable for recreation. The foreshore between Barrack Square and the Narrows Bridge is being redeveloped into an attractive venue for residents and visitors, with cafes, commercial properties and park facilities.

However, the council is very conscious of its environmental obligations and the importance of maintaining and enhancing its natural assets. It adheres to a framework laid out in the City Environment Plan 2005/08. The development at Point Fraser on the city's eastern approaches is an example of the City of Perth's progressive thinking in environmental management. The project incorporates design elements to reduce pollution in stormwater run-off into the Swan River, while creating an aesthetic new recreation facility.

The City is also very protective of its heritage. It has taken the lead by funding the restoration and refurbishment of one of the city's oldest buildings, the Perth Town Hall, at a cost of more than $10 million. The Perth Town Hall now meets the requirements of a 21st-century public meeting venue. The council has introduced a number of programs – such as grants, rate relief, a heritage award and plot ratio incentive schemes – to ensure that its significant old buildings are not sacrificed in the name of progress.

The City of Perth funds its initiatives from a range of income streams. Its revenue base exceeds $100 million, with 43 percent of that derived from rates and 30 percent from parking fees. The City is the biggest provider of car-parking spaces in Perth through its parking business City of Perth Parking (CPP). It has 35 off-street car parks containing 11,400 off-street bays. It also maintains 6,000 on-street, or kerbside, bays. In July 2004, CPP opened the 1,500-bay Convention Centre Car Park after negotiating a 99-year lease. The council's decision to invest $45 million in this project was based on a commercial investment in city parking and to stimulate economic development and vitality by ensuring the Perth Convention Exhibition Centre was built within the City's boundaries.

However, it's not all work and no play. The council supports and hosts many of Perth's major cultural and sporting events. It presents the annual Australia Day Skyworks celebrations – the country's biggest – and is a major sponsor of the Perth International Arts Festival, Opera in the Park and the Northbridge Festival. It also conducts its own events, including school holiday activities.

It is a difficult juggling act, but the City believes it has the right mix to satisfy competing interests so WA residents and visitors have a capital they can work, live and play in.

Above left: The historic Perth Town Hall stands proudly amid progress.
Above: The iconic Swan Bells tower.
Left: Tranquil Queens Gardens.

LIONEL SAMSON & SON

Starting a business is tough at the best of times. But try doing it after sailing half way around the world to a newly discovered land with just a few dozen strangers for company and nothing but barren land at your destination.

What may sound like a scene from an intriguing reality TV show is actually the real life story of Australia's oldest family business – as old as Western Australia and still going strong.

Lionel Samson and Son – its building still in WA's historic Fremantle port district – has been operating since 1829.

The pioneering Samson family's fascinating story began on a cool winter's day in August 1829, when the small barque Calista reached the shores of the Swan River colony on Australia's west coast.

It had been an arduous five-month journey from England, through the world's most treacherous oceans. But for the 73 weary travelers, the final destination would not have offered much relief.

They were among the colony's first settlers, landing on the beach near Fremantle's Arthur Head with nothing but their tents to keep them dry, 14 horses and 200 sheep.

Aboard the Calista were brothers Lionel and William Samson. The prominent members of the London Stock Exchange and high society had decided to leave London after receiving glowing reports of the new land from Captain James Stirling, who had explored the area in 1827 and was to become its first governor.

Despite the harsh environment and no infrastructure, the brothers began building a merchant business. They bought land and gradually expanded their enterprise to become the backbone of trade in the colony.

Their business L & W Samson dealt in wine, spirits and wholesale groceries using merchandise they had brought with them and later sourced from visiting ships.

As the colony grew, the business expanded to export sheep, cattle, horses and dried fish. The brothers also became heavily involved in the administration of the colony. Lionel was appointed postmaster at Fremantle and William the government auctioneer.

When William left to follow business pursuits in Adelaide, Lionel brought his sons – first William then Michael – into the business, renaming it Lionel Samson & Son.

"The company, from its very beginning, was based on respect and ethics and this environment was the ingredient that has seen the grand old company grow and diversify," Steve Samson, Lionel Samson's great-great grandson said.

"Over nearly two centuries ownership of the business has been retained by eight family groups, descendants of Lionel Samson. This is rare indeed."

Right: The directors of Lionel Samson. Below right: Lionel Samson premises in Fremantle.

PLANTAGENET WINES

Plantagenet Wines has established an enviable reputation for producing award-winning premium West Australian wines.

Western Australia's Great Southern is perhaps one of the finest wine regions in Australia – its vineyards rivaling even France for the quality of red and white wine varieties.

The rich soil had long been an undiscovered secret but a few visionaries realised the potential of the area some time ago.

The first among them was the young and vibrant Tony Smith who, in 1968, planted an experimental vineyard on his Bouverie property.

Today, Plantagenet Wines produces three labels – the premium Great Southern Plantagenet Range, Omrah and Hazard Hill.

But the road to success has not been as smooth for Plantagenet as its produce. After many trials and tribulations, including some untimely pruning by a flock of stray sheep, the first grapes were picked in 1974. The resultant wines were the first Plantagenet shiraz and cabernet.

The shiraz was tight and lean and showed the distinctive spiciness of the region while the cabernet was robust. This inspired Mr Smith with the confidence and enthusiasm to establish the first commercial winery in the Great Southern region.

In 1975 he bought an apple packing shed in Mount Barker and converted it into a winery. Its first vintage was produced under the guidance of winemaker David McNamara.

As the winery grew, vineyard plantings expanded. In 1998 the aptly named Rocky Horror vineyard was established 15 kilometres south of Mount Barker.

The land was originally dotted with large subsurface boulders as big as small cars. These were crushed and added back to the soil over two years, creating the perfect environment for vines to struggle out of the ground.

"We went a little overboard two decades ago when we first came across the vineyard Omrah, so named after the striking and luxurious SS Omrah," Plantagenet Wines marketing coordinator Mary-Anne Parker said.

"In the early 1900s, the ocean liner spent 18 years sailing to and from Albany in Western Australia, ferrying settlers and soldiers to and from our shores.

"Our Omrah range of wines embodies all that is best from Western Australia – a pioneering spirit built from youthful enthusiasm and a lot of character."

In 1994 Lionel Samson and Son, Australia's oldest wine and spirit merchant company, purchased a share in the winery. Plantagenet's winemaking expertise and Lionel Samson and Son's extensive experience in wine and spirit sales proved the perfect blend. This was the start of a successful relationship between the Great Southern premier winery and the old Fremantle merchant company.

Expansion continued throughout the '90s in both the winery and the vineyards. Rosetta vineyard was established in 1999 taking the total vineyard plantings to 130 hectares.

Plantagenet has established an enviable reputation for producing premium wines over its 30-year history, winning more than 350 trophies and medals.

Above right: Wyjup vineyard at Mt Barker.
Right: Plantagenet's vintage crew.

SADLEIRS TRANSPORT

Right: Sadleirs operational area at Kewdale.
Below: Family members and directors of Sadleirs, Steve Samson and Ian Cook.

Long before rail lines were built on the west coast of Australia, a local transport company was doing its best to get those in the fledgling colony and their businesses moving around the state and beyond.

Sadleirs Transport, or R.C Sadleir as it was then known, was a pioneer on the West Australian business scene when it was established in 1895 as a Fremantle customs, shipping and transport business.

The company thrived in one of the harshest business environments in the world – through colonisation and two world wars – to become a modern day industry leader still growing after 111 years.

Sadleirs steadily grew with Western Australia and its developing transport industry – from shipping to trucking and rail, then air and electronic communication.

For the first 60 years, shipping was the only form of interstate transport available on the west side of the country but Sadleirs worked hard to develop a reliable local distribution network. The company always embraced challenges, finding new ways to go forward – from the days of the horse and cart to jet transport.

Sadleirs' potential as a strong business ally was quickly recognised by Australia's oldest family business, Lionel Samson and Son. The merchant company was looking to expand its operations when it took an interest in R.C. Sadleir in 1937.

In the mid 1950s Sadleirs expanded into interstate transport and in 1969, following the introduction of standard gauge rail, moved its head office from Perth to Kewdale.

The company offers a superior level of service across Australia because it has modern infrastructure and importantly, loyal and dedicated staff, according to Sadleirs managing director Ian Cook.

"Our emphasis on customer needs has been the focus of our business since it started over a century ago in Fremantle," Mr Cook said.

The interstate transport network means the company can move just about anything around the country. This is reflected in its motto "small enough to care, large enough to cope". In Western Australia it offers an integrated logistics solution with warehousing and container handling facilities on site.

Today Sadleirs is rated as one of Australia's leading independent road and rail freight forwarders with a computer-linked network of company-owned depots across the nation.

SADLEIRS INTERNATIONAL

More than 100 years ago, when Western Australia was just a tiny Swan River colony, transporting goods overseas took months. Today, the French could be savouring the state's famous lobsters just hours after they had been caught in WA waters.

The Sadleirs group has been a pioneer in the transport industry right from the beginning, growing into a large global transporter through Sadleirs International.

The company is driven by the philosophy that efficient and reliable freight forwarding is crucial to modern business, no matter what the destination around the world.

It does not just import and export goods door-to-door anywhere in the world, it specialises in the providing hassle-free transport solutions for even the most challenging jobs.

"At Sadleirs International we have earned a reputation as one of Australia's most professional international freight forwarders and customs agents," general manager Alun Powell said.

"It's our strategic approach to the handling of goods that makes us different. We call it 'freight forward thinking'.

"In fact, we specialise in unusual and challenging projects – from rock concert staging to rally cars, live lobsters to ripe strawberries, industrial equipment to diamonds."

The company can even help move an entire drilling platform or a thoroughbred racehorse to a new home on the other side of the world.

"With this kind of cargo you want solutions and the special care and attention that only Sadleirs International can deliver," Mr Powell said.

"Our special projects team has an unsurpassed reputation in the successful project management of some of the world's most demanding and difficult freight forwarding jobs."

This ability to answer any challenge stems from the company's beginnings in 1895. The Sadleirs group was established in the growing Swan River colony where transport of any kind was difficult. The company had no choice but to always think outside the square to provide the best possible service to clients.

Armed with this experience, the team at Sadleirs International makes understanding client needs a priority to help find better freight forwarding solutions.

"We untangle red tape, handle difficult goods with ease and meet virtually impossible deadlines," Mr Powell said.

"Sadleirs International is part of a nationwide transport group that has been around for more than a hundred years and has its own road, rail and specialised haulage infrastructure."

A global network of specialist partners and state-of-the-art computerised tracking systems backs up the entire operation.

"We are now an international business but we continue to play a strong part in the local community and are active members of industry bodies," Mr Powell said.

Whether it's handing live food, complex machinery or the humble unaccompanied baggage, Sadleirs International is building on more than 100 years of experience to get the job done efficiently and on time.

THE SWAN BREWERY

Named after the captivating black swans synonymous with Western Australia and its rivers, Swan Brewery was founded in 1857. Over 150 years, the brewery has established itself as one of the state's most iconic and successful businesses – an integral part of the WA landscape.

The Swan Brewery, an independent brewery under the Lion Nathan umbrella, produces up to 100 million litres of beer annually and is home to WA's most adored beer brands.

Together with traditional favourites Swan Draught and Emu Bitter, Swan also brews leading national beer brands from the Lion Nathan portfolio including Tooheys New, Tooheys Extra Dry, XXXX GOLD and Hahn Premium Light. Additionally, the brewery is responsible for distributing international premiums Beck's and Heineken, together with the James Squire range of craft beers.

In 2007, Swan celebrates its 150-year anniversary. Since its humble beginnings all those years ago, Swan has undergone a radical transformation, growing in size from a family-owned business established by an early WA settler and former school teacher, Frederick Sherwood, to being an important part of Australia's second largest brewing group and ASX100 company, Lion Nathan.

While not the first brewery in WA, Swan quickly established itself as a brewing force in the state through its flagship brand, Swan Draught. In its first century, Swan acquired the Lion, Kalgoorlie, Castlemaine and Emu breweries and by the end of the 1960s owned more than 120 hotels throughout the state. In 1982 Swan became a wholly owned subsidiary of Alan Bond's Bond Corporation and in 1992 achieved its current status as an independent brewery under the Lion Nathan umbrella.

As ownership changed hands and Swan grew, the brewery moved location several times. Originally situated at Sherwood Court, Swan relocated to the old Emu Brewery site at Crawley in 1938 and then to its current site at Canning Vale in 1978.

However size and location aren't the only things that changed. Working practices have also been transformed significantly.

In the early days, brewery workers enjoyed a regular supervised intake of beer – two glasses before starting work at 7.30am, two at the 10am morning tea break, two at lunch, two at around 3pm, and another two before leaving for the day. This system apparently encouraged punctuality in the staff.

Today, Swan Brewery employs 370 staff (none of whom drink before or during working hours) making up just over 10 percent of Lion Nathan's trans-Tasman workforce. Together with providing the safest and healthiest workplace possible, Swan prides itself on offering staff a chance to be the best they can be, to really make a difference, and to have a great time doing it.

While a lot has changed since Swan's early days, it is the brewery's core values of integrity and passion that remain unchanged.

Along with Lion Nathan's other breweries including Tooheys in New South Wales, Castlemaine Perkins in Queensland and the South Australian Brewing Company, Swan Brewery is about 'making the world a more sociable place'.

Regional director for WA, Frank Arangio, believes the secret to Swan's longevity has been its commitment to this vision and, in particular, to meeting the needs of WA drinkers.

"Beer is a social product and our drinkers are passionate about their choice of brands. Our job is to make sure they can always get their hands on the product they want at the time, and in the place, they want it," he said.

"Obviously, in the early days, WA's population was small because when the brewery opened the state was merely 30 years old. Today, we have two million people in WA, all with unique needs and wants.

"As time has passed, we have obviously introduced more brands to our offering. So while Swan and Emu led the charge in the early years, we're now seeing consumer repertoires increase and are responding to that increase with a portfolio of products that includes local, national and international brands.

"Interestingly, the premium beer market in WA is growing faster than most other states across the country. This shows what a truly diverse and cosmopolitan community we have in the West."

Right: Swan Brewery, Canning Vale open 1978.

Integral to Swan's ongoing success in the state is not only its product offering, but its commitment to local sporting, cultural and charitable events, as well as the community.

In the sports arena, Swan and Lion Nathan are supporting rugby at all levels through Tooheys New. As well as being the naming rights sponsor of the Tooheys New Super 14s Rugby Tournament, Tooheys New also supports WA's inaugural team in the competition, the Western Force, and grass-roots rugby. The brewery's long association with horse racing also continues, with XXXX GOLD being a major supporter of all regional turf clubs including Bunbury, Kalgoorlie-Boulder and Broome.

Culturally, Swan and Lion Nathan support the Perth International Arts Festival through international offering Beck's, while supporting Big Day Out and Rock-iT through Tooheys Extra Dry. When it comes to charitable donations, Swan goes the extra mile, running 90-minute fundraising tours of the brewery, the proceeds of which are used to support a number of local causes. Swan also supports the Variety Club of WA.

At a community level Swan is acutely aware of its responsibilities and, as part of the Lion Nathan group, is committed to being a responsible producer and marketer of products that contain alcohol. The group's newly launched BeDrinkAware.com.au logo will be progressively introduced to all packaging and marketing materials and the company continues its commitment to the Alcohol Beverages Advertising Code and Complaints Management System, as well as the independent pre-vetting of all its advertising.

Though more than 90 breweries have come and gone across the state, Swan Brewery remains, injecting close to $45 million into the WA economy annually. It is a leading force in the state's brewing history, and is set to continue making history well into the future.

Above: The Original Swan Brewery 1857, Mounts Bay Road, Perth.
Top: From the days gone by, custom filling wooden kegs with Swan Draught.

FREMANTLE PORTS

Fremantle Ports operates from an Inner Harbour at Fremantle and an Outer Harbour, 20kms south at Kwinana.

The Inner Harbour handles most of the container trade for WA, as well as general cargo trades, cruise liners and navy visits. The Outer Harbour is one of Australia's major bulk cargo ports handling grain, petroleum, liquid petroleum gas, alumina, fertilisers, sulphur and other bulk commodities.

Fremantle Ports operates the Kwinana Bulk Jetty and the Kwinana Bulk Terminal at Kwinana, providing facilities to handle a range of imports and exports. Alcoa, BP and Co-operative Bulk Handling also operate cargo-handling facilities in the Outer Harbour.

About 27 percent of the nation's wheat and some 19 percent of the nation's alumina is exported from Kwinana.

The successful port operation is strategically managed by Fremantle Ports, a West Australian government-owned organisation that operates as a commercialised trading enterprise.

Fremantle Ports chief executive Kerry Sanderson says the port has experienced strong growth in container trade, which in 2004/05 was about four times the level in 1990/91. Trade in new motor vehicles and bulk materials is also increasing. This has required an upgrade of infrastructure, with Fremantle Ports undertaking its biggest capital works program in decades.

Right: The Kwinana Bulk Terminal is one of two bulk handling facilities operated by Fremantle Ports in the Outer Harbour.

Opposite page: (top) View of the Inner Harbour at sunset and (bottom) Fremantle Ports' container trade continues to grow strongly.

A major project completed in the Inner Harbour in 2006, was the construction of the $32 million North Quay rail link and rail terminal to service the container trade.

"The dual-gauge rail link will improve freight efficiency and help reduce the growth in port-related truck traffic on connecting roads as trade grows," Ms Sanderson said.

About two thirds of the funding for the new rail infrastructure has come from the state government, with a contribution of $9.5 million from the federal government under the AusLink program.

In the Outer Harbour, the upgrading of the Kwinana Bulk Terminal has been tackled as a top priority to service the needs of the HIsmelt commercial pig iron plant and other customers. The work has included upgrading and extending Fremantle Ports' conveyor systems and installation of a new high performance bulk unloader.

Fremantle Ports provides and maintains shipping channels, navigation aids, wharves, road and rail infrastructure within the port area, moles and seawalls and other port infrastructure. It also owns and manages the Fremantle Passenger Terminal on Victoria Quay. Other services provided include port planning, ship scheduling and berth allocation, port communications, pilot transport, mooring, security services and ensuring emergency response capability.

Fremantle Ports is a creative, dynamic organisation that aims to facilitate trade in an environmentally and socially responsible manner to efficiently meet the needs of its customers and other stakeholders now and in the future.

Ms Sanderson said the organisation's broad objectives were to ensure that port services and facilities were reliable and competitive and met customers' needs.

"We work closely with our customers to facilitate trade opportunities and we are strongly committed to continuous improvement of our services to provide value for our customers and provide for long-term business sustainability," she said.

Fremantle Ports is one of only a few organisations in WA to be recognised at award level by Business Excellence Australia for high level performance in business improvement and strategies for long-term success. This awards program is designed to foster organisational excellence and achievements, and the evaluation process is the most rigorous of awards programs available to organisations in Australia.

Business Excellence Australia judges stated: "Fremantle Ports has demonstrated its commitment to leadership through innovation and best practice, resulting in leading-edge customer management processes, excellent standing within the industry and an excellent understanding of its market."

Ms Sanderson said Fremantle Ports was committed to operating in a sustainable way, integrating economic, environmental and social considerations into its business approach.

"As well as our certification to international quality and environmental standards, achieving a better understanding of community priorities and perspectives and operating as a good corporate citizen is an important part of this," she said.

"Stakeholder support for the working port remains strong, and we will continue to work to minimise port impacts while adding value to our community."

As well as being a busy working port, Fremantle is one of WA's most popular visitor and tourist attractions. Implementation of the Fremantle Waterfront Masterplan to revitalise the western end of Victoria Quay and improve links between the waterfront and Fremantle's central business district is well underway. The new Maritime Museum and O'Connor ferry landing are part of this development and an exciting commercial precinct with offices, retail, cafes and restaurants is planned.

When the busy Inner Harbour at Fremantle reaches capacity, additional container and general cargo berths will be needed at Kwinana to take the overflow trade, with both harbours then continuing to operate together. Based on Inner Harbour capacity, Fremantle Ports' proposed expansion of container and general cargo port facilities is still some years away from being required. However, significant progress has been made towards obtaining approvals for the overflow facilities.

Fremantle Ports' expansion plans have been developed through very detailed and wide-ranging studies over more than two decades. This is a complex project, one of great importance to WA's ongoing economic growth.

CITY OF BELMONT

The City of Belmont has created a vibrant place of opportunity that combines attributes of Perth's city and country lifestyles close to the Swan River.

Whether you are looking for a place to live or invest, develop your business, or just to enjoy your lifestyle, the City of Belmont has opportunities ready to be discovered.

The City of Belmont is a vibrant community located six kilometres from Perth's central business district, along 11 kilometres of Swan River frontage.

There has been unprecedented growth in the City in recent years, with significant commercial and residential developments and the establishment of a number of new industries.

Belmont's business precinct is less than 10 minutes from Perth. Affordable land and proximity to air, rail and road transport arteries have drawn businesses to the area. There are also many opportunities to build, develop or lease business premises in Belmont and car parking is in greater supply than the City, allowing for a significant cost advantage.

Almost 3,000 businesses are based in the City of Belmont, ranging from the headquarters of multi-national companies to micro and home-based businesses. This has created a strong employment market, with nearly two jobs for every resident of working age in the City of Belmont. These figures are surpassed only by the Cities of Perth and Fremantle.

A framework has been created to ensure that the area's residents and businesses can work together to create a dynamic community. The council has paved the way for successful commercial developments by creating a plan for a "mixed business" precinct with clear guidelines and increased certainty for developers.

While Belmont is close to the CBD, the area also offers a mix of unique amenities usually associated with country or coastal communities.

Ascot Racecourse and the surrounding residential stables precinct is a distinctive feature of the City. This is the only place in metropolitan Perth where a suburb has been planned specifically to allow horses and

residents to co-exist. The racecourse attracts tourists to the area and adds a level of excitement and entertainment, especially during the Ascot Summer Racing Carnival.

Belmont is also proud to have its own marina at Ascot Waters. The Marina Village has a mix of commercial properties and prestigious homes with waterfront apartments and townhouses, which allow residents to moor their boats just seconds from their front doorsteps.

As inner-city property values escalate, the Belmont residential sector is also going through a significant level of redevelopment and improvement, bringing increased population opportunities.

Land in the City of Belmont along the Swan River, known as the "Golden Mile" is an area to watch for development.

This keenly sought after pocket of land is located between Great Eastern Highway and the Swan River, from the Graham Farmer Freeway to Ascot Waters. The development of this land will result in a stronger waterfront identity for the City, as the potential of the river frontage is realised. It will re-define and re-value the foreshore and surrounding suburbs.

Belmont has a rich multicultural history and was the location of some of Perth's first market gardens in the 1890s. This history can be seen throughout the City, for example one of Belmont's premier parks, Tomato Lake, is named after the location where tomatoes were first grown in 1914.

Belmont was originally established as the Belmont Road Board in 1898 and has since grown to a thriving municipality of more than 30,000 inhabitants, known as the City of Belmont. Belmont comprises the suburbs of Ascot, Redcliffe, Belmont, Cloverdale, Kewdale and Rivervale.

The City of Belmont joined an elite group of companies and government bodies in 2006 by achieving international quality assurance accreditation.

Below right: Quality business developments continue to grow in the City.
Below: Ascot Waters housing.

This means that the City of Belmont's core processes are recognised as being consistent and of a high standard.

Belmont also has a focused strategic plan which sets the direction for the City. Along with this, the fully integrated marketing strategy has enabled Belmont to solidify strong branding and image as the City of Opportunity. This certainty and confidence continues to attract businesses and residents to prosper in the City.

There is a great sense of community in Belmont, with strong business networks and also lively centres for community gathering. Faulkner Park is a hub of activity, with a feature playground and a skate park that regularly hosts Extreme Sports Fests for the young people of the area. The Ruth Faulkner Library, Council Civic Centre, Belmont Oasis Leisure Centre and Youth and Family Service Centre are also located close by, making it convenient to access services and recreation.

Council has a recreation strategy in place to encourage residents and those working in the City to enjoy fitness and recreation nearby. This culture of activity also flows through to the schools, who work closely with the council to ensure local young people are provided with recreation and sporting opportunities.

There is an extensive network of public parks and open spaces throughout the suburbs, with a park located within a three-minute walk from most homes.

These include the picturesque Garvey Park on the riverfront and Adachi Park with its mix of Australian and Japanese influences.

Other landmark locations within Belmont include the domestic and international airports, Kewdale Freight Terminal and Belmont Forum Shopping Centre.

The City's residential land densities encourage families into the area and new medium-density developments close to major transport routes and community facilities are now also attracting executives, singles and retirees.

Plans for Belmont's future will continue to take advantage of its central location, scenic natural features and thriving business networks.

The City of Belmont is living up to its identity as a place where opportunities continue to grow.

Above: Adachi Park with a mix of Japanese and Australian influences.

Left: One of the City's popular events.

Bottom: Garvey Park river frontage.

WRAY & ASSOCIATES

Protecting intellectual property (IP) is vital and the best way to do this is by enlisting trusted, professional help. Wray & Associates is a West Australian firm of patent and trade mark attorneys which specialises in looking after some of the brightest ideas in the state.

Founded in 1920, it is WA's biggest independent, locally-based firm of patent and trade marks attorneys, according to the chairman of partners, Peter Caporn.

"The firm commenced operation in 1920 when a newly registered patent attorney, Peter Bonnerup travelled from Melbourne to Perth to establish the firm P.M. Bonnerup & Co," Mr Caporn said.

"Mr Bonnerup practised in Perth until his retirement in 1955 when Reg Wray took the reins. In 1959 the firm was renamed R.C. Wray & Associates.

"Reg retired in 1985 and a year later the firm changed its name to Wray & Associates. It currently has seven partners, 23 professional staff and is Western Australia's leading firm of patent and trade mark attorneys."

And while the practices may have changed over its many years in the business, the firm's main focus remains the same – to help establish and protect the intellectual property rights of its clients.

This service includes: assisting local clients in obtaining protection for their intellectual property worldwide; representing overseas clients' interests in Australia; and protecting clients' intellectual property rights in Australia and overseas.

Wray & Associates offers wide-ranging and substantial technical expertise embracing mechanical engineering, electrical engineering, computers, physics, chemical engineering, inorganic and organic chemistry, mineral processing, pharmaceuticals, molecular biology, biochemistry, microbiology, plant biotechnology and plant breeders rights.

The firm also offers services in all areas of patents, trade marks, domain names and registered designs. With an extensive local and interstate client base, it has considerable experience in all aspects of drafting and prosecution.

"We provide services in the fields of licensing and assignment of products, the defence of our client's rights, and we have wide-ranging expertise in defending or challenging the validity of other's rights. We also offer searching services as well as extensive monitoring services for competitive patent and trade mark applications," Mr Caporn said.

Right: Wray & Associates professional staff can assist with a wide range of IP needs.

The firm's services are diverse, reflecting the changing needs of its clients. One of its areas of expertise is the prosecution of patent, trade mark and design applications. The firm will pursue the grant or registration of rights by addressing any issues raised by IP Australia, the body governing intellectual property applications.

"Several of our professionals have experience as patent examiners so we are well placed to understand the intricacies of examination from an examiner's point of view," Mr Caporn explained.

"Additionally, we understand that defending your hard-earned IP rights is crucial to your business success and thus we will act on your behalf in oppositions being conducted against other parties before IP Australia."

The firm's experienced patent attorneys and technical assistants have specialist expertise covering most areas of science and technology. They have the necessary experience to understand inventions and designs and to prepare accurate patent specifications.

"The technical expertise of our staff covers mechanical, chemical and electronic engineering, physics, computing, chemistry and biotechnology," Mr Caporn said.

"Our technical illustrator is able to prepare high-quality drawings for design and patent applications and, of course, we can prepare and lodge trade mark and domain name applications that are most appropriate for your needs."

Wray & Associates has access to a wide range of international databases covering all areas of science and technology. It also has on-line access to the public records of IP Australia and therefore to the latest status details available.

"We are able to offer searching services that include searches for the existence, status and scope of particular patents, registered designs and trade mark registrations; the novelty of an invention or industrial design; any potential conflicts that may arise by the marketing of a particular product; any potential conflicts that may arise by the utilisation of a particular trade mark; and the registrability of a trade mark," Mr Caporn said.

"We are also able to conduct general awareness and literature searches simply for information or research purposes.

"We can quickly obtain copies of the full text of published patent specifications, published design registrations and captured details of trade mark applications and registrations from Australia and any other country."

The firm can provide professional opinions on the patentability or registrability of inventions, designs and trade marks. It can also give professional infringement opinions, both from the perspective of the alleged infringer and also from the perspective of the owner of the rights.

The watching service allows the client piece of mind, thanks to the firm's ability to maintain watches on any particular patent, trade mark or design application or registration, and to provide regular reports on their progress.

"If you are concerned about staying abreast of the activities of your competitors, this is a service that is often useful," Mr Caporn explained.

"We can also undertake specific technology watches to inform you of patent applications published or accepted in a field of interest."

Wray & Associates can advise on various aspects of the preparation and relevance of licences and assignments of intellectual property rights.

The firm can handle the renewal of all registered intellectual property rights, ensuring timely and effective preservation of IP.

"Our computer database maintains records over extended periods (indefinitely for trade mark registrations) and automatically issues reminders prior to due dates," Mr Caporn said.

Wray & Associates even provides a draftsman service to promptly produce high-quality illustrations for any patent or design requirements for virtually any country around the world.

"Our draftsman is trained and qualified in technical illustration and often travels to our clients' premises to gain an insight into a device or product before commencing his drawings," Mr Caporn said.

Wray & Associates also takes its community role seriously by sharing its vast knowledge with academics and research groups.

The firm's partners and other professionals regularly address such groups as part of their educational programs.

"Education in our field of expertise is an essential ingredient of the value-added service that we provide to our clients," Mr Caporn said.

"We are willing to provide speakers at any functions and for any organisations which are similarly committed to the education of the public."

JACKSON MCDONALD

West Australian law firm Jackson McDonald has been helping the state's business sector grow for more than 80 years.

In a global economy where relationships across borders are becoming increasingly important, a West Australian law firm is successfully going against the trend of national mergers.

One of the state's oldest and highly respected law firms, Jackson McDonald, has chosen to stay local. It has established strong associations with other highly respected law firms around Australia and overseas to service its clients' needs, wherever they may arise.

Building on an 84-year history, one of WA's biggest commercial law firms has been nurturing a highly skilled and experienced team that is acutely aware of local client needs, while at the same time adopting global best practice in law firm service delivery.

For Jackson McDonald, providing a high quality service and being client focused remains a winning formula.

Excellent local knowledge and insight into WA business practice, the political environment and the nuances of the local regulatory regime, give Jackson McDonald a leading edge.

Below: Jackson McDonald has been playing a key role in WA's rapid infrastructure and construction growth.

Jackson McDonald is a firm of choice for clients in industries such as energy, mining and resources, property, building, construction, insurance and financial services.

Of particular current significance, the dynamic energy sector in WA faces many challenges brought about by legal and regulatory changes. These include increased retail contestability in electricity and gas, the disaggregation of monopoly providers, a consolidation of ownership in energy assets and a shift toward national regulation.

Jackson McDonald has played a key role in drafting and advising on the restructuring of the energy industry since the mid-1990s, with the introduction of open access regimes for gas and electricity and the gas licensing regime. Recently these roles have included the gas retail market rules and key electricity reform instruments.

The state's resources sector, driven by demand from China, has experienced huge growth with flow-on benefits spilling beyond the mining industry. It has resulted in an increase in commercial property transactions in WA, with very strong CBD office demand both for buying and leasing. The retail sector has been a star performer in property portfolios.

Land tenure and title security is a fundamental aspect of major resource projects and Jackson McDonald's expertise extends into all aspects of due diligence and implementation for such projects – whether for participants, investors or financiers.

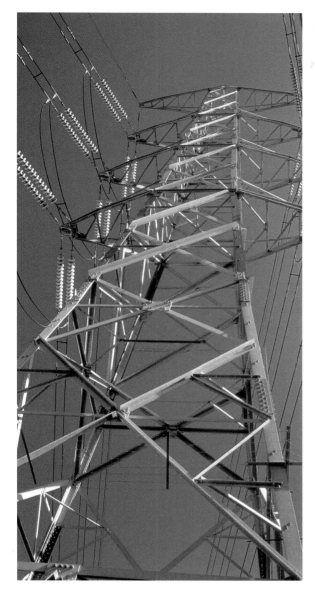

The big private and government sector investment in major infrastructure and construction projects in these sectors and across the state is likely to continue.

The Jackson McDonald building and construction team expects to continue to play a key role in WA's rapid infrastructure and construction growth, providing advice on contract selection, preparation of construction contracts, tenders, contract administration, claims management and dispute resolution.

The firm is also active in all facets of corporate advice and transactions, including capital raisings, business sales and purchases, mergers and takeovers and provides due diligence, taxation, intellectual property, corporate governance, competition and trade practices, planning, insurance, insolvency and workplace relations advice to clients.

The firm's lawyers have represented clients in all courts and tribunals and in alternative dispute resolution such as arbitration, conciliation and mediation.

The firm devotes substantial time and resources to the betterment of the profession through active involvement in the Law Society and relevant tertiary education programs. The firm's alumni have gone on to populate the judiciary, the ranks of independent barristers and many company boards.

Jackson McDonald prides itself on investing in the training and development of its people to ensure they are abreast of industry changes, their legal knowledge is current and they are continuing to develop their client service skills.

The lawyers are trained and mentored by partners and senior staff and secondments are offered to enhance awareness of the client's commercial environment. Jackson McDonald also plays an important part in the WA community. In addition to partners and staff being personally involved in numerous community organisations, the firm offers pro bono legal work to charitable organisations and supports them through fundraising activities. The firm has for many years also sponsored the WA Citizen of the Year Award in the professions category.

More than 80 years of experience has taught Jackson McDonald that smart people, working closely with their clients and supported by modern high quality systems, achieve the best outcomes for clients. The firm's whole approach to managing the practice is geared to achieving just this.

Jackson McDonald will continue to put its primary focus on clients and their interests, as it has done for the past 84 years, and continue to invest in the development of the legal profession in the state.

Above: Working closely with clients to achieve the best outcomes remains an important focus.

Top left: Since the mid 1990s Jackson McDonald has been heavily involved in the energy sector in WA.

Jackson McDonald services:

- Alternative dispute resolution
- Banking
- Building, construction and engineering
- Commercial
- Competition and trade practices
- Corporate transactions
- Energy and competition policy
- Environment and planning
- Estate planning and estate administration
- Financial services
- Government
- Insolvency and reconstruction

- Insurance
- Intellectual property
- Liquor licensing, hospitality and tourism
- Litigation
- Mining and resources
- Occupational safety and health (OS&H)
- Property and leasing
- Taxation
- Technology
- Town planning
- Transport
- Workplace relations

RSM BIRD CAMERON

When it comes to a balance sheet, reasons for employing the services of RSM Bird Cameron are all in the black.

The accounting and corporate advisory firm combines the personalised service of a local business with the strength of the large international firm backing it.

National chairman Kim Hutchinson said RSM Bird Cameron's association with RSM International allowed it to offer a seamless service internationally. "We can meet clients' global requirements from over 70 countries around the world," he said.

"When clients cross borders, our independent network enables the RSM team to assist them using common standards, a common approach, co-ordinated teams, the highest level of international service standards and total commitment to finding the right solutions.

RSM International member firms are linked by the same IT systems, by common training and a close understanding of each other.

This structure and our entrepreneurial spirit, mean RSM professionals can move quickly to provide solutions."

Edgar Woolcott founded RSM Bird Cameron in March 1922 as The National Service Company, offering tax advice for small and medium-sized local businesses.

RSM Bird Cameron now offers a range of services including business solutions, assurance and advisory, corporate consulting and succession planning. It also provides traditional accounting services such as general accounting, taxation compliance and statutory reporting for regional and metropolitan sectors.

There are 28 RSM Bird Cameron offices across Australia, 17 of those in WA. However, despite the firm's international and national links, RSM Bird Cameron's head office is in Perth.

"We feel that keeping our head office in Perth is another thing that differentiates us from our competitors," Mr Hutchinson said

"Our roots are in WA and we feel that by not giving into the pressure dictated by large companies to be based over east, we are able to keep our clients and our staff happy."

The firm, which started with two employees in 1922, now has more than 650 employees nationally and 330 staff in WA.

RSM Bird Cameron has overcome many challenges in its 84-year history.

While many businesses struggled in the 1930s and 1940s because of world events such as World War II and The Great Depression, the firm continued to grow.

Sir Cyril Bird joined the firm in 1931 and worked to develop and expand the business.

"It wasn't an easy time. The firm reduced salaries and cut other areas of expenditure to survive, but because of clever management it pulled through and continued to develop," Mr Hutchinson said.

In the 1950s, the firm moved from the corner of William Street and St Georges Terrace into new premises at 18 St Georges Terrace.

Mr Hutchinson said RSM Bird Cameron started its international association in 1985 when the firm became a member of Dunwoody Robson McGladrey & Pullen.

*Right: Gary Chappell,
director of WA Regions.
Far right: Kim Hutchinson,
national chairman.*

It officially became RSM Bird Cameron in 2000 when it became a core member of RSM International, the sixth biggest accounting and consulting firm in the world.

The firm is involved with local and national community and business initiatives.

"Having a presence in metropolitan and regional areas, the firm is able to recognise young achievers in all parts of the state," Mr Hutchinson said.

"One major sponsorship initiative is our support of *WA Business News*' 40under40 Awards."

RSM Bird Cameron's own achievements and commitment to clients has been recognised in the 2005 and 2006 BRW-St George Client Choice Awards.

The awards are given based on a survey of more than 10,000 people who rated over 150 professional services firms. Beaton Consulting ran the survey, with respondents typically chief executives, chief financial officers and in-house lawyers.

In 2005, RSM Bird Cameron received three awards – for Best Mid-Sized Accounting Firm, an Attribute Award for Exceptional Service and Best WA Firm.

This success was repeated at the 2006 awards, when RSM Bird Cameron won the Best Mid-Sized Accounting Firm award for the second year

running. It also received an Attribute Award for Outstanding Client Service and another state-based award.

"We were delighted to be recognised in the awards for the second year running," Mr Hutchinson said. "I believe that these awards reflect our national commitment to excellence in client service as well as the dedication of our staff that provide this service.

"As 2005 was the first year of the awards, we were truly delighted to receive three accolades. To be this successful for the second year running demonstrates that our commitment of delivering exceptional service to clients holds true."

For the past 12 months, RSM Bird Cameron has been actively seeking ways to differentiate itself in the middle market and a key strategy has been to ensure staff and clients are informed about the firm's strategic developments and future directions. The future for RSM Bird Cameron is bright, with the firm continuing to grow strongly with the economy.

Above: The Bird Cameron building at 8 St Georges Terrace. Opened by Sir Charles Court in 1989.

LOTTERYWEST

In the 1930s, Western Australians were facing serious hardship as the Great Depression hit hard. Faced with widespread poverty, the government passed legislation in 1932 creating a state lottery to raise funds for public hospitals and charities.

People paid 2/6 for a chance to win £1,000 in the very first lottery run by the Lotteries Commission, drawn on March 21, 1933. The holder of winning ticket number 55383 was 13-year-old Joan Smart of Cottesloe, who announced that she would use the prize to further her education.

About 55,000 people had bought a ticket for the draw and, in the pursuit of a windfall for themselves, had raised $3,000 for Western Australians in need.

For many years, draw lotteries, or 'charity tickets', were the Lotteries Commission's only lottery product. But in February 1979, Western Australians were introduced to a game which would capture their imagination like no other – Lotto.

Today, Lotterywest offers a range of lottery products, ranging from 'scratchies' (Scratch'n'Win instant lottery tickets) to Powerball, and Western Australians are passionate lottery players. Lotterywest consistently records the highest sales per capita of lottery games of any Australian lottery and, when it comes to Lotto, has one of the highest sales per capita in the world.

This unique public sector organisation has become one of the world's most successful lotteries, providing 100 percent of its profits to the community – around $1.5 billion in the last decade alone. WA's Lotto players can buy a ticket which gives them a chance at prizes of $20 million or higher. And a single draw can raise more than $5 million for the community.

A business which can make millionaires overnight has a special glamour but as CEO Jan Stewart explains: "It's the drive to continue to raise funds for our community that motivates those of us who work at Lotterywest."

Lotterywest is overseen by a board of business and community leaders who ensure the organisation operates on commercial principles to provide the best return to the WA community. In 2005, Lotterywest's sales totalled more than $520 million, over $280 million was won by players and more than $160 million was given to the Western Australian community.

The money is shared well. Each year, a fixed percentage of proceeds goes to the public hospital system and organisations in the sports and arts sectors. WA's public hospitals are the biggest lottery winners of all, with around $80 million provided for the state's public health services each year.

A wide range of arts groups, including the West Australian Symphony Orchestra and the West Australian Ballet and Opera companies, share the $10 million provided by Lotterywest to ArtsWA. The same amount is distributed to sporting associations including the WA Institute for Sport. The rest, about 40 percent, is distributed by Lotterywest through grants to community organisations.

Lotterywest does not think in terms of 'charitable causes' but rather of responding to community hopes and aspirations. In all, around 1400 grants by the Lotterywest grants team are recommended for approval by the Minister for Government Enterprises every year. Grants are given for a wide variety of initiatives ranging from equipment for local children's play groups, to support for Perth's Australia Day celebration, 'Lotterywest Skyworks' now watched by 50 percent of all Western Australians; from the construction of 23 'Lotteries Houses' around the state providing shared

facilities for community organisations, to innovative recreation programs for people with disabilities.

Lotterywest is the principal partner for the Perth International Arts Festival and a vital source of funding for Western Australia's local film and television industry. And Lotterywest plays a crucial role in supporting important community events such as the annual 'Anzac Day' commemoration as well as many programs run by and for Indigenous Australians. Lotterywest is also a major source of funds for conservation projects and for the preservation of heritage sites and buildings.

As Ms Stewart says: "It would be hard to find someone in Western Australia not touched by Lotterywest."

Of course, every dollar provided to the community must first be raised through the sale of a Lotto ticket, 'scratchie' or other lottery game.

Lotterywest sells its products through a network of more than 600 small businesses throughout WA, many of them neighbourhood newsagents and local stores. For almost all of them, lottery games are a critical component of their business. Lotterywest's retailers share more than $40 million in commission from the sale of lottery products each year, and Lotto and Scratch'n'Win are key drawcards for their outlets.

Others who benefit from Lotterywest's business include the organisation's many business partners and suppliers. As well as international suppliers of the gaming technology and the interstate manufacturers of the Scratch'n'Win tickets, these include local businesses such as Lotterywest's advertising partner, printers and shopfitters. In all, around $20 million each year goes to Lotterywest's suppliers.

At the heart of the lottery business is of course the dream of a life-changing win. Every year almost $300 million in prize money is shared between WA's lottery players. And among them will be the lucky few who have done what the rest us of dream of doing – winning the magical Division One Lotto prize.

Top left: As the 'principal partner' to the Perth International Arts Festival, Lotterywest helps bring some of the world's finest arts to Western Australia every summer.
(PHOTO COURTESY OF THE UWA PERTH INTERNATIONAL ARTS FESTIVAL 2006, PHOTOGRAPHER TONI WILKINSON)

Above: Fabio the pony is one of hundreds of animals rescued from mistreatment by RSPCA: an organisation which has been equipped with the help of Lotterywest grants.

Left: Stepping out – Lotterywest grants support a wide range of community projects such as the stunning Lotterywest Federation Walkway in historic Kings Park.

HBF

HBF's vision is to create and maintain Western Australia's most valued membership organisation through the active provision of a unique combination of personalised products, services and benefits.

Indeed it is HBF's focus on its members – and not on profits – that has made HBF one of WA's most highly regarded organisations. As a not-for-profit mutual organisation, HBF aims to serve and care for its members and help ensure their long-term physical and financial wellbeing. It is HBF's mutual structure that is its essential difference from most other insurers, as it exists to help members, not to drive profits for shareholders.

HBF members benefit from a comprehensive range of insurances, including hospital, ancillary, car, home, contents, personal valuables and travel. In recent times, the organisation has begun providing a range of financial services, including financial planning and life insurance.

And, as WA's largest membership organisation, HBF plays an important role in empowering members with information to help improve their lifestyle, advocating on key issues of community concern.

HBF's mutual structure is its essential difference from most other insurers, as it exists to help members, not to drive profits for shareholders.

HBF was established during the Second World War in a time of shortages, rationing and increasing regulation to help ordinary Perth residents pay their hospital bills.

Launched on April 1, 1941, it was originally known as the Perth Metropolitan Hospitals Benefit Fund and only covered Perth hospitals.

It was built on the tradition of friendly societies and early hospital schemes and was initially administered by a provisional committee of management with backgrounds in WA's metropolitan hospitals.

The original constituent bodies of the fund, the Perth, Fremantle and Children's Hospitals, appointed an equal number of representatives to the committee with an independent chairman.

Since its inception, the fund has grown from strength to strength, quickly becoming the leading provider of health insurance in WA.

By the end of June 1944, after only its third year of operation, MHBF's membership had exceeded 50,000 members. With the fund prospering, its health cover was extended for treatment in all WA hospitals.

In October 1945, the word 'Metropolitan' was removed from the fund's name to emphasise that coverage included all West Australian hospitals.

By 1954 HBF had more than 250,000 members and 103 staff.

During the 1960s and early 1970s it took over several smaller funds and its membership grew to almost 650,000 by the mid 1970s, which was about 65 percent of the West Australian population.

With the introduction of the federal government's Medibank in 1975, the health insurance industry changed significantly, which resulted in HBF membership dropping to more than 430,000 by 1977. HBF had to find new ways to offer its members the highest quality service that was also competitive in an ever-changing market and political climate.

Therefore in the late 1970s it launched its first comprehensive advertising campaign, which saw member numbers increase greatly in 1982. The introduction of Medicare in 1983 resulted in membership numbers dropping by 11.6 percent within a year. Partly in response to this, HBF diversified into general insurance in 1983, offering home, building and car insurance and, in 1986, travel insurance. In the early 1980s HBF's branches grew from five to ten, including several regional outlets, and formed an important point of contact for members.

In 1998 HBF formed a strategic partnership with the metropolitan St John Ambulance Fund. It also heavily promoted the federal government's new Private Health Insurance Incentive Scheme, which encouraged greater health insurance membership. Both of these initiatives saw HBF's membership jump from 570,000 in 1997 to more than 848,000 the following year.

The introduction of the federal government's 30 percent private insurance rebate in 1999 followed by its Lifetime Health Cover in 2000 – to promote private health insurance – saw HBF membership swell to a record 900,000.

However, record membership numbers also coincided with record claims.

In recent times external factors, such as rising costs, new technology and the ageing population, have placed great pressure on the health insurance industry. With forecasts predicting a continuing increase in claims in the future, HBF had to examine alternative sources of income.

Below: For more than a decade Mike Gurry has been the managing director of HBF and spearheaded its diversification program.

Having developed a successful general insurance business, HBF decided to diversify into financial services to give the organisation a broader base for the future and help keep premiums to a minimum.

In 2004 HBF offered financial planning and in 2006 it launched life insurance, with plans to offer other financial services to give members an even greater range of products and services.

Today the organisation has about 660 staff and 19 branches around WA as well as its head office in Murray Street, Perth.

The fund looks after WA people in many different ways.

To help tackle one of the biggest health concerns to emerge in our community in recent times, HBF launched HBF Action for Healthy Kids in 2003.

The initiative saw HBF enter into partnerships with key community organisations committed to finding a solution to childhood obesity. The program also sponsored events that encouraged Western Australians' involvement in physical activity, especially children.

Heading the program was HBF family doctor, Duncan Jefferson, who provided health information and advice to members and the community.

In recent times HBF's member advocacy program has begun expanding, especially into areas that impact on both the physical and financial wellbeing of members.

People at HBF have always been genuinely concerned about doing the right thing for the members and the WA community.

In the past ten years, HBF, with the help of its staff, suppliers and members, has raised more than $860,000 for charities. Annually HBF employees donate about $50,000 to local charities through a payroll deduction scheme plus an additional $50,000 through fundraising activities.

Although HBF has undergone considerable growth in the past 60 years, its community focus and strong ethic of service excellence has not changed.

It has always maintained a unique culture that has inspired both loyalty and commitment from staff and members.

There is no doubt that HBF's long-term success and focus on people has provided the organisation with a solid foundation for the future.

Above: An organisation that puts people before profits, HBF's service centre network is a valuable point of contact for members.

Top left: HBF family doctor, Duncan Jefferson, and Western Australian School Canteen Association's executive officer, Robin Bromley, together produced the HBF Healthy Eating at School Guide.

Left: the HBF Telethon Toddle is part of HBF's Action for Healthy Kids program. The event encourages young children to be physically active as well as raise funds for children. The inaugural event in 2005 raised more than $40,000 for Channel 7's Telethon.

WESTRALIA AIRPORTS CORPORATION
– PERTH AIRPORT

Perth Airport is at the centre of Western Australia's booming economy. A conduit linking all business sectors, it literally brings together the people and resources that make WA the nation's economic benchmark.

Westralia Airports Corporation Pty Ltd (WAC) is a company on the move. Entrusted with the enormous task of operating Perth Airport – WA's most iconic transport infrastructure hub – it truly is an industry leader.

As lessee of Perth Airport under a 99-year agreement with the federal government, WAC works in daily partnership with some of the world's best known brands. Home to such companies as Qantas, Singapore Airlines, Virgin Blue, Emirates and Air New Zealand, it is Australia's closest major airport to South-East Asia, Europe and Africa.

Perth Airport is the international, domestic and regional gateway to Western Australia. Catering for commercial passenger, freight, charter and private aircraft, it is the nation's fourth largest airport in terms of passenger traffic. With the capacity to meet both the current and projected aviation needs of the state well into the 21st century, the airport is a mere 12km from the central business district and the site encompasses 2,105 hectares. In 2003, Economics Research Australia studied the economic significance of Perth Airport finding that it provides around 16,800 jobs and contributes $850 million in wages to the state's economy. The report estimated that all airport associated activities generated approximately $2.2 billion a year or 3 percent of gross state product (GSP) for WA.

Following privatisation in 1997, the airport has experienced continuing upward growth in passenger numbers. At present, nearly seven million passengers depart from or arrive on WA's doorstep per year, making a critical contribution to the state's economy. In the financial year 2004/05 passenger growth was in excess of 7.5 percent, making it the busiest on record for the airport.

Below: Entrance to Terminal 1 (International).

Since 1997, WAC has enjoyed considerable growth and success under the experienced leadership of chief executive officer Graham Muir.

With over 17 years experience within the aviation and tourism industries, including roles with Federal Airports Corporation at Melbourne Airport, Mr Muir brings to WAC a significant depth of experience. Assisting the industry to prosper is a vital element of Mr Muir's role and he is chairman of the Perth Convention Bureau and director of the Tourism Council of Western Australia.

Mr Muir believes the organisation's vision to be – "a world class airport and a great place to do business," – has a tangible impact on operations.

"The staff of Westralia Airports Corporation strive to make our vision a genuine blueprint for corporate action, including undertaking a record capital works programme which will deliver benefits to all airport customers," Mr Muir said.

The stunning refurbishment of Terminal 1 (International), including 38 new check-in counters, was completed in August 2005 and represented a $25 million investment by the corporation. Security is of major concern to the travelling public and indeed for WAC, and it therefore remains a critical corporate priority. As a result, the terminal refurbishment included installation of an automated baggage handling system and an in-line checked baggage security screening system. Other service improvements include major runway upgrades to facilitate wide-bodied aircraft, a relocation and refurbishment of the passenger screening point at Terminal 1, refurbishment of the passenger screening point at Terminal 3 (Domestic) and the introduction of new retail dining and convenience outlets including Dome Café, the New Orbit Inn, Fresh Connections and the Relay and Hub Convenience store at Terminal 3.

Perth Airport's outstanding commitment to customer service has twice been formally acknowledged by the industry's peak body – the Australian Airports Association. As winner of the Major Airport of the Year Award for two consecutive years in 2003 and 2004, Perth Airport has carved a unique reputation for itself in a notoriously changeable industry.

A vocal advocate promoting Western Australia as a destination of choice for international and domestic travellers, WAC works closely with the state government in air service development and in attracting more airlines to the state. The corporation has been a proud sponsor of the key industry awards program since 2000 – the Western Australian Tourism Awards. In 2005, WAC took this commitment to the next level by becoming the event's partner sponsor.

While Westralia Airports Corporation core business will always centre on the domestic and international traveller, in recent years it has diversified its business base with significant success.

One example is the corporation's pursuance of a property development strategy, investing over $50 million in major commercial and industrial (non-aviation) development. Perth Airport has over 700 hectares available for a range of property development and caters to more than 200 tenants including the Australian Quarantine and Inspection Service, Star Track Express, Australia Post, Cummins, Officeworks, Atlas Copco, Western

Power, DHL and many other national and international household names. WAC has recently released Kewlink East which is an 85 hectare estate and home to the giant Woolworths and soon-to-come Coles Myer regional distribution centres. Significant further development is planned for the airport which has fast become the location of choice for many major Western Australian companies, particularly those requiring large lot sizes.

Westralia Airports Corporation remains committed to ensuring all development on its landholdings is undertaken in an environmentally sensitive manner. The Perth Airport Environment Strategy, approved by the federal government, is used to manage the impact of all airport activities on the environment.

Over 300 hectares of the Perth Airport estate has been set aside for the conservation of natural environmental values. The reserves contain important areas of good quality vegetation, plant species listed as rare by the federal government, significant wetlands, habitat for local fauna and sites of cultural significance. An active management program has been implemented to enhance the reserves through various activities, such

as feral animal and weed control, rehabilitation planting, seed collection and the maintenance of fencing. The reserves are closely monitored to ensure they are properly managed to maintain the natural environmental values. Perth Airport has also convened an Environmental Consultative Group to allow stakeholders, such as community groups, to have an active voice in the management of the conservation areas.

While WAC has achieved many major milestones in the nine short years since privatisation, it has also faced some significant challenges. National and global events such as September 11, the SARS crisis and increased global terrorism have made the need for organisational adaptability greater than ever.

When asked if the fluid nature of his industry was a cause for concern, Mr Muir's response was swift and emphatic.

"We operate in a dynamic industry that can literally change overnight. I love this business and have every confidence that Westralia Airports Corporation will continue to respond effectively to every challenge presented to us."

Top left: International Terminal apron.

Left: Check-in counters at Terminal 1 (International).

Above: Aerial view of Perth Airport, showing proximity to the Perth CBD.

WOODSIDE

It's possible that about three-quarters of the intellectual capacity of Australia's oil and gas industry is centred on Milligan Street at the western end of Perth's St Georges Terrace.

Not in ties and coats but in an almost universal uniform of open-neck shirts, tailored slacks and sometimes jeans. These men and women work with the companies exploring for and producing oil and gas and the service companies that support them. They mingle in the restaurants, cafes and shops below their offices, in the buildings that soar above the Terrace and look across the Swan River to Rottnest Island and the Indian Ocean.

It is one of the most stunning vistas of any city which makes the concentration not really surprising. Nearly two-thirds of Australia's oil and gas production comes from Western Australia, much of it from the North West Shelf Venture which is Australia's biggest single resources development.

The figures are mammoth. The Shelf gas project involves an investment calculated in today's dollars at more than $A19 billion. Its current expansion will take annual capacity to more than 16 million tonnes and make the development one of the world's top five LNG producers.

Projects such as these don't just occur because of happenstance. They are an amalgam of resources, opportunity, markets, financing and, above all, intellectual effort.

Development of the oil and gas industry in Western Australia during the past 50 years is closely associated with the growth of one of the companies whose headquarters lies in the industry's intellectual quadrant – Woodside.

And the fact that Western Australia is now experiencing the richest period in its history, surpassing the gold boom of the 1890s, is due in no small part to changes wrought as a result of Woodside's evolution from a struggling exploration minnow to a highly profitable, world-ranked oil and gas producer.

The company began life in 1954 as Woodside (Lakes Entrance) Oil Co NL, an explorer registered in Victoria, named after a small coastal town in a region that had been known for decades for its seeps of oily residues that promised a lot but delivered little immediately after the Second World War changed forever the world's energy priorities.

Woodside was among several small stock exchange-listed companies – penny dreadfuls – that hoped to strike it rich.

Hopes and reality were far apart and it seemed likely Woodside and its promoters would be consigned to history's dust cart but for one small political accident.

It was not in Victoria, with its market close to the world-scale oil and gas reservoirs of Bass Strait, that Woodside was to make its name.

It was in the challenging northern offshore waters of Western Australia that its destiny was found.

These days, Woodside manages the huge North West Shelf Venture which processes gas and oil for domestic and export sale at an onshore processing plant at Karratha, more than 1500km north of Perth.

Customers throughout the south-west of WA rely on venture gas for cooking and electricity. In Japan, millions of gas and electricity customers rely on regular supplies shipped in dedicated tankers from the shelf.

It is a far cry from 1963 when Woodside was awarded huge exploration acreage off the north-west coast of Western Australia for the princely sum of 100 pounds. That's about the closest you'll come to happenstance in the Woodside saga.

In the 1950s, Western Australia had evidence of oil at Rough Range, in the Carnarvon basin 65km south of Exmouth, but it was too small a discovery and in too remote an area to be considered commercial.

But government geologists were convinced the area's geology was attractive and they argued the government should offer exploration acreage in a bid to attract real investment in exploration and capitalise on the renewed interest in Australian oil and gas as a result of discoveries in Bass Strait, off the Victorian coast.

The hope for interest from the international majors was dashed and it was only the struggling minnow, Woodside, which was interested. And so it was

Night life: The Karratha onshore gas processing plant lights up as the sun sets over the Pilbara coast. It is Australia's biggest gas plant.

awarded exploration permits covering 367,000sqkm of the geologically unknown ocean in the north-west of Western Australia.

Linking with British groups Burmah Oil and Shell, Woodside formed a joint venture to explore an area one and a half times bigger than its home state.

In 1968, they found the Legendre oil field and then in 1971 Woodside discovered the Scott Reef, North Rankin and Angel gas and condensate reserves.

North Rankin provided the basis for what became known as the North West Shelf Venture, which obtained government approvals in 1979.

During the following two years, the Western Australian government contracted to buy 20 years supply of natural gas from the project to supply Perth households and industry and commerce in the south-west of the state.

During the same period, eight Japanese gas and electricity utilities, among them the biggest energy suppliers in the world, contracted to buy LNG from the venture to satisfy the needs of a huge number of their customers in Japan.

This dry recitation of corporate history masks a period of intense excitement as Woodside and its partners made discovery after discovery, spawning headlines across the country and huge sharemarket activity.

Almost by accident, Western Australia had become part of the LNG industry – the fastest growing energy business on the planet.

The turquoise blue of Roebuck Bay near Broome, the mangrove-fringed islands of the Bonaparte Archipelago off the Kimberley coast, the burgeoning ports of the Pilbara and the atomic blast sites of the Montebello Islands became synonymous in the 1970s with the successful search for oil and gas.

Then, as now, it was oil that was the focus of the search, particularly against the background of political events in the Middle East that had sent oil prices soaring and limited supplies to the United states sparking fears about the security of energy that continue to be reinforced today.

But it wasn't oil that triggered billions of dollars of investment in one of the most challenging environments in the world. It was gas.

Aside from being remote, lacking population and industry, the ocean off the Pilbara and Kimberley coasts was frequently lashed by cyclones.

Transforming the gas reservoirs deep beneath the seabed was going to take more than just the application of techniques used elsewhere in the world.

It was going to take massive capital, precious little of which Australia had in the 1970s. It was going to take large markets and greater demand than Australia could provide. And it was going to require brain-power, in the short term and for decades, in a country that wasn't geared to train the geologists, petroleum engineers, construction engineers and technologists that would be needed.

Australia had no knowledge of LNG development and only limited experience of exporting hydrocarbons to an increasingly aggressive world market.

And, of course, Woodside had no experience of managing major projects.

That meant it had to find corporate partners – ones with access to funds, technology and global markets.

Enter companies such as BHP Billiton, Shell, BP and Chevron as well as the Japanese giants, Mitsubishi and Mitsui. They accepted Woodside's role as project operator, without the company ever having produced a barrel of oil or a gigajoule of gas. That they continue to do so today, speaks volumes for the transformation of Woodside over the past 50 years.

In the early days, the fledgling company was continually under pressure to produce results that demonstrated its capacity to learn on the job as its team directed development of a world-scale resources project with the advice and strong support of international partners, particularly Shell.

Above: Lorne Bussell — one of the more than 100 people on the North Rankin platform which contains more steel than the Sydney Harbour Bridge.

Right: Getting there — crews do two-week offshore shifts and are ferried to and from Karratha by helicopter, a trip that takes about 30 minutes.

After 10 to 15 years of trying to run the project from Melbourne, Woodside's operational and corporate headquarters transferred to Perth to be closer to the action.

It was a move that has had an intense impact on Perth and encouraged other companies to follow.

International political intrigue marked the first attempts to convert the North West Shelf Venture's discoveries into commercial sales. The partners had hoped to win contracts to supply LNG to Japan in 1975 but lost out to producers in Malaysia who already had experience in corralling the vast amounts of finance and technology required to convert gas below the sea into an easily transportable commodity.

Bob Rowland, who's now in his 21st year as a Woodsider — after six years on secondment to the North West Shelf from BHP — says it's hard to recollect just how the challenges of the 1970s and 1980s were met when looking at things from today's perspective.

But he is clear that without the foresight and enthusiasm of the then Western Australian Premier, Charles Court, who ensured that the state government bought natural gas from the Shelf partners and who also built the pipeline system that delivered it to the domestic market, the project would have stalled.

Sir Charles, now well into his 90s, is still passionate about the North West Shelf — a passion that once led him to suggest that a critic of the domestic gas contract should be charged with treason for doubting the capacity of the state to pay for it.

At 53, Mr Rowland has spent most of his working life with Woodside and its projects. As project development manager he is at the centre of Woodside's future while drawing strongly from its past.

"Because Woodside has so many projects, we have 750 project personnel employed, of whom half are Woodside employees and half are contractors," he says, adding that more will probably join by the end of the year.

While Woodside has moved on from being manager of a single project — this year it has begun producing oil from the Chinguetti field off Mauritania in West Africa — Mr Rowland notes that the initial facilities on the Shelf are coming to the end of their original design life.

That produces new challenges, not necessarily directly associated with producing oil and gas.

When the first offshore production facility was built, the North Rankin platform was one of the biggest of its type in the world, up-scaled from North Sea experience to handle a once in a 100-year cyclone.

"The Rankin platform was designed with a gap above the waves of 23 metres," says Mr Rowland, pointing out that since it was installed in the early 1980s it has survived three storms of greater magnitude than those it was planned to handle.

North Rankin was designed using data that spanned 100 years of weather history, some good, and some bad. Experience shows that the data was insufficient – not dissimilar to the experience of offshore projects elsewhere in the world such as last year's hurricanes in the Gulf of Mexico that devastated New Orleans and savaged oil and gas installations.

Mr Rowland says the Shelf is the most important of the 15 or so projects that Woodside's development teams are associated with today, simply because it is the heart of the company and will remain so for years.

"North Rankin A is an ageing facility with a design life that expires in 2009," says Mr Rowland. "We are in the design concept phase for North Rankin B, with a decision on the concept required later this year so that it can be online in 2009 to 2010.

"What's changed? Well, in the first place it's our concern for people. If we are designing platforms with a greater air-gap than the 23 metres on North Rankin A, then elsewhere on the Shelf we have to put in a bigger air-gap on North Rankin B which will predominately house people, not equipment. It's a simple part of risk management and that's what's changed a lot."

Because North Rankin B is likely to contain all the accommodation from North Rankin A, its design is also causing a re-think about what will occur on the original platform. It seems more than likely that as well as producing oil and gas it will remain as the drilling and production platform, sending out long-reach wells of 8km or more into the Perseus gas reservoir which, with North Rankin and Goodwyn, now provides most of the gas that is exported to Japan.

As a measure of the continuing exchange of information across the Woodside business, Mr Rowland notes that the project team on Chinguetti will move on to the project team on North Rankin B, which is in its formative stages.

Their work will extend the life of North Rankin A to 2035, a timeframe that demonstrates at the very least huge confidence that the petroleum province has sufficient gas reserves to meet demand.

The original reservoir at Rankin is in natural decline and Goodwyn is showing signs, as expected, that it is beginning to decline too.

Mr Rowland tells a wonderful story about the discovery of Perseus, which indicates that perhaps not all the science and technology in the world can overcome the need to respond to the human factor.

"We had the big North Rankin reservoir and next door the Goodwyn field," he says with infectious enthusiasm.

"We were drilling long reach wells from the North Rankin platform to recover gas from the reservoir. I think we had the long-reach North Rankin 21 well that went out through the reservoir.

"After a while we found that the recovery in this well never declined, so we said to the exploration boys to have a look.

"So Perseus was actually discovered by a development well on North Rankin A," he says with a sly dig at the glamorous exploration side of the business.

Like all true oilmen, Mr Rowland likes to project a little mystery, not dissimilar to those in the gold industry who believe Kalgoorlie's fabulous Golden Mile has a parallel lode.

Having found a reservoir between Rankin and Goodwyn, he says he wouldn't be surprised if Woodside finds another gas field on the other side of Rankin. Time, and more exploration, will tell.

After a quarter of century of living in Perth, Mr Rowland is hooked and says many of his colleagues share his view that there's no better place to be. Many have travelled around the world and are back in Perth for their second or third stint at Woodside or with other oil companies using Perth as a headquarters for Australian operations and a base for international activities.

"It's an easy place to live compared with many oil and gas centres," he says. "Perth's a place that's not only interesting for the work, it's got a relaxed lifestyle and good feel about it that's attractive for a lot people in our industry."

Increasingly, it seems he may be right. Perth is Australia's most multicultural capital, in part because of the demand for skilled labour from the resources sector. And more and more, these skills come from all around the world.

The oil and gas sector is no exception, with several projects expected to come into production in the next decade attracting personnel from almost anywhere. But that doesn't mean ignoring the locals.

A recent top-level management decision has resulted in Woodside adopting a bigger role in educating indigenous populations in its domestic and international operations.

That, says Mr Rowland, has been one of the changes of which he's been proud to be part. "Woodside keeps re-inventing itself about every 18 months so you're never short of something challenging to keep you busy," he says.

Challenges at the moment include the proposed Pluto LNG project. It is set to become the fastest LNG development in the world, with the gas field

on the North West Shelf discovered in April 2005 and with production slated to begin in 2010.

There's also the inaugural LNG delivery to China's Guangdong Province under the first contract that the Chinese signed to supply LNG.

Woodside is operating in Mauritania and Algeria, exploring in Libya and in several other African countries, taking part in the continued development of the Gulf of Mexico and operating in the Timor Sea, all a long way away from its Victorian birthplace.

Woodside's chief executive, Don Voelte, is also a long way from his native Nebraska, but distance doesn't seem to faze him as he travels the world extolling the skills and people that helped the company become a preferred partner in the oil and gas business.

A long-time international oil industry executive, Mr Voelte says something about the Woodside culture is different and it may have something to do with the mix of cultures and experiences of its workforce in Perth.

It is something that makes the company an attractive partner in other countries and something on which the CEO is keen to capitalise.

But for Bob Rowland and his mates, living and working in a Perth-based company is not something they are ready to give up any time soon.

SKYWEST AIRLINES

Below: F100 wing tail.

Opposite page: (right) Skywest cabin crew Karen and James; (bottom) Skywest cabin crew member Rebecca assists passenger Geraldine.

Long distance travel is an essential part of living in Western Australia.

The sheer size of the state – covering almost half of the Australian continent – poses many obstacles for local travellers and tourists.

But WA's premier regional airline, Skywest, is helping to bring the remote and popular parts of the state closer together.

For more than 42 years, the award winning carrier has met the needs of millions of travellers, flying them in comfort and style across the vast state, Northern Territory and to Bali.

It is an essential link for regional communities, tourists and businesses.

Skywest has forged a peerless reputation since its inception as Carnarvon Air Taxis in 1964. It has grown from humble beginnings through incorporation as part of Ansett Airlines, to listing on the Australian Stock Exchange.

Skywest's fleet of Fokker 50 turbo prop and Fokker 100 jet aircraft is based at Perth Airport's domestic terminal.

Each year, it flies more than 320,000 people across the state and the NT with more than 220 flights each week. Its regular ports include Albany, Esperance, Geraldton, Carnarvon, Exmouth, Broome, Darwin, Kalbarri, Kalgoorlie, Karratha, Kununurra, Monkey Mia and Port Hedland.

Skywest chief executive officer Johanna Ramsay said the airline has answered the challenge posed by the complexity of long distance travel in WA.

"In addition to our scheduled services, Skywest's regional charter service caters for the specific needs to corporate, government, mining and resources clients, operating aircraft charter services to the state's most remote locations," Ms Ramsay said.

"Skywest is big enough to provide a full range of airline services but small enough to maintain flexibility.

"We are uniquely equipped to meet customer needs. Our airline is geared toward catering for the business and leisure air travel needs of West Australians, as well as our interstate and international visitors."

Aside from providing a crucial regional transport service, the airline ensures its customers travel in absolute comfort, even while flying over some of the world's most isolated and harshest terrain.

"We pride ourselves on our superior in-flight service, offering on every flight great tasting, premium Dome plunger coffee, hot meals, full bar service and the most spacious economy legroom of any airline in Australia," Ms Ramsay said.

Skywest planes are more likely to depart on time and the airline consistently rates as Australia's most punctual, as measured by the Department of Transport and Regional Services.

It recently reaffirmed its status as WA's premier regional airline, winning the Major Tour and Transport Operator category for the second year running at the 2005 WA Tourism Awards.

But the road to success has not always been easy. Like many WA grown businesses, Skywest has had to overcome some unique challenges.

In 2001, this journey took Skywest close to being a casualty of the collapse of the national airline Ansett – the parent company of Skywest for more than 14 years.

It was only after intense lobbying by loyal staff for a government grant that Skywest was resurrected later the same year, its business flourishing ever since.

One of Skywest's first milestones was the launch of its service from Perth to Albany in 1974. Its potential for growth was soon realised by Ansett, which bought the WA airline in 1987.

Skywest began flying its first Fokker 50 plane in 1994 – expanding to five aircraft two years later.

Following Ansett's collapse, Skywest quickly asserted its commitment to the local market, thanks mainly to a terrific show of support from customers, many in some of the state's most isolated areas.

A major growth spurt began in 2002 with Skywest modernising its booking system and opening a call centre. It also took delivery of its first Fokker 100 jet, significantly cutting travel time to some of WA's most remote destinations.

In 2003, Skywest began flying to Broome – a popular tourist destination in WA's north.

Pilbara to Bali flights followed in 2004, as well as Darwin, Port Headland, Karratha and Newman routes. The airline launched the inaugural Skywest Showcase – a one day workshop bringing together tourism suppliers, operators and direct front line sellers from across the five regional tourism zones of WA and the Northern Territory.

The same year, Skywest also listed on the Australian Stock Exchange and won its first Major Tour and Transport Operator WA Tourism Award.

In 2005 the Kununurra service began and the airline won a government tender to deliver regular services to key coastal areas.

This year, Skywest began flying to two more tourism hot spots – Kalbarri and Monkey Mia.

"We are working hard to build Skywest's jet fleet to become a 'jet airline' and become a major contributor to the growth of regional tourism in WA," Ms Ramsay said.

"Our vision for the future is to be recognised as the leading regional airline in Australia.

"To achieve this, Skywest has an ongoing commitment to provide a tourist travel experience at a world class standard."

THE DOWERIN GWN
MACHINERY FIELD DAYS

The Dowerin GWN Machinery Field Days event is the biggest and most important showcase of agricultural machinery and associated equipment in Western Australia, with the distinction of also being the oldest field day in the state, entering its 42nd year in 2006.

The community-owned event is run by a board under the trading name of Dowerin Events Management Incorporated, with two full time staff – a CEO and an events coordinator – reporting monthly to the board.

More than 400 volunteer staff from communities throughout rural WA, work for an hourly rate, paid to their pre-nominated charity, club, school, or association.

The event had its genesis on May 10, 1964, when the Dowerin Progress Association held a meeting to try to find ways of preventing Dowerin becoming a ghost town (a not uncommon fate of Wheatbelt communities across Australia) and also raise funds to build a dam to help reticulate the town sports oval and tennis courts. One of those attending had just returned from visiting a field day in Orange, New South Wales and suggested Dowerin hold a similar event.

Communication and distance had always been problems for wheat belt farmers and the idea of having a working machinery event, where they could compare rival equipment under identical conditions, was very appealing and the idea was accepted. The inaugural field day was held on Friday September 3, 1965, with some 20 exhibitors and 2,000 visitors, leading to calls for the field day to run for two days the following year. Accommodation was a concern, however the surrounding towns benefited, as people booked rooms in places such as Northam, Goomalling and Wongan Hills – a tourism-related positive for the towns.

The original objectives of raising funds for a dam and grassed sports grounds were achieved very quickly and the event then assumed responsibility for loan repayments on the town swimming pool. At the same time, catering for the large numbers of visitors had become a problem and a catering committee was established.

A decision was taken to pay volunteer workers for their services, by way of a cheque to the local organisation of the volunteer's choice, for example the local fire service, sporting club, school, or other association. It was and continues to be a masterstroke in distributing much needed funds to deserving organisations across WA's wheatbelt.

The Dowerin Field Day event continued to expand, with permanent power being supplied to many sites in 1975 and the eventual building of an indoor basketball arena, which could be used for the Family Interest Display section during field days. By 1991, exhibitor numbers had risen to 503, with in excess of 34,000 visitors. In 1992, the regional television broadcaster, Golden West Network (GWN), came on board as the naming rights sponsor, a position they proudly retain to the present day.

It had become an icon event, both for the farming community and the people of Perth.

In 1996, the event won the prestigious Significant Local Festivals and Events category of the West Australian Tourism Awards and proceeded to take out the same category in the national awards. The event won again in 1997 and 1998 and was then rewarded with a permanent place in the West Australian Tourism Hall of Fame.

From a humble suggestion for raising funds to water a tennis court, the Dowerin GWN Machinery Field Days had become the biggest rural event in Western Australia, a "must attend" showcase for people from all walks of life.

Turning to the present day, and the town of Dowerin, (settled 1897), lies approximately 160 kilometres north-east of Perth, in the heart of the central wheatbelt. Farming methods have changed dramatically in the past 40 years and the combination of bigger machinery, plus the amalgamation

Below: Dowerin Shire CEO Les Crighton and Field Days chairman Mike Irvine.

of smaller farms into larger properties, has seen populations dwindle. It is now commonplace to sit in a tractor and watch it steer itself by GPS. A USA manufacturer has just released a tractor with no cabin or provision for a human operator. One machine now does the work of three tractors and three operators – in half the time.

The net effect to Dowerin is that, while the local volunteer base has dropped, volunteers now come from rural communities across Western Australia, all benefiting from the three-day event.

People often think of farmers as being small business people. Nothing could be further from the truth. Farms these days involve million dollar-plus land values and often, machinery purchases exceed $500,000. Big, sophisticated business by any measure and time is a precious commodity, which is why the annual event continues to be a vital part of the farming calendar – a unique opportunity to see and acquire information on machinery, production methods and associated farming lifestyle products in one arena.

There is a strong social element to the field days, a chance for farmers and their families to catch up with neighbours from far and wide, while the event also serves as a way for exhibitors to give something back to their customers and the wider community.

As broadacre farming evolves and other influences make themselves felt, the Dowerin GWN Machinery Field Days continue a natural evolution. Technology is an essential part of broadacre farming, with the use of computers and satellite beamed information and these days, computer displays share space with farm machinery.

Lifestyle farms are moving closer to centres such as Dowerin, it's possible to run many consultant type businesses from rural areas and already the sea change lifestyle has seen smaller tractors dominate farm machinery sales across Australia (2005). Viticulture and olive tree farming have reached the wheatbelt, as has the production of trees, such as Blue Gums and Paulowina.

The Dowerin GWN Machinery Field Days will continue to encourage exhibitors to meet the trends, expectations and needs of the many diverse groups who rely on the annual event for information on the very latest developments in machinery, computers, finance, cropping and even information on schools and fashion.

The board has now approved the design and construction of a hotel / motel training complex, which will be used for the launch of new equipment and machinery, further cementing Dowerin's position as the pre-eminent centre of excellence for machinery.

Above: Harvesting demonstration at Dowerin (1966).

Middle: 1973 – from little things, big things grow.

Top: Aerial view of Field Day activity.

CONSOLIDATED MINERALS LTD

Consolidated Minerals Limited is a diversified West Australian resources group focused on the exploration, development, production and export of high-grade minerals to global markets from three mining centres located across the state.

Consolidated has grown through a combination of exploration success, organic expansion of its operations and acquisition to become one of Western Australia's leading mid-tier resource groups – employing more than 450 people including onsite operators, transport contractors and company staff.

Listed on the Australian Stock Exchange, where it is included in the benchmark ASX Standard & Poors 200 index, Consolidated also has secondary listings on the Alternative Investment Market of the London Stock Exchange and the Frankfurt Stock Exchange.

It has a strong production base in the supply of carbon and stainless steel raw materials through its manganese, chromite and nickel divisions and is developing new businesses in zinc, copper and iron ore.

Consolidated has a clear vision to continue to achieve sustained growth and maximise returns to shareholders through capital growth and dividends by:

- leveraging off the strong cash flows of its steel and stainless-steel related businesses;
- undertaking growth or acquisitions where value-accretive;
- attracting the highest quality and most experienced management and operational personnel;
- maintaining a focus on Australian, particularly West Australian, resource projects.

The engine room of the company's growth to date has been Consolidated's successful West Australian manganese operations at the Woodie Woodie mine in the state's Pilbara region. This operation is owned by its wholly-owned subsidiary, Pilbara Manganese.

Woodie Woodie, about 400km south-east of Port Hedland in the Pilbara, has a secure position as a reliable supplier of up to one million tonnes per annum of high-grade, low-phosphorous manganese ore to markets in Asia and Europe, representing a sustainable 10 percent share of the world market.

Consolidated's high quality product, Pilbara Manganese, is recognised in world markets because of its high manganese content and low phosphorous and iron levels.

About 90 percent of manganese ore worldwide is consumed in the steel industry, the majority of which is processed initially into manganese alloys. Manganese is an essential and non-substitutable input to the steel-making process due to its ability to desulphurise steel and prevent-oxidation, and its alloying properties (to improve toughness and hardness).

Consolidated maintains an intensive exploration program at Woodie Woodie to further expand the company's reserve and resource inventory and increase mine life.

Consolidated's second Pilbara operation, held through its wholly-owned subsidiary Pilbara Chromite, is the Coobina Chromite Project, 80 kilometres south-east of Newman. It produces 250,000 tonnes per annum of 42 percent chromite ore.

Coobina ore is renowned as lumpy, hard chromite, differentiating it from many of the world's friable chrome ores and making it an ideal blending ore in alloy smelters.

More than 80 percent of chromite ore is used in the production of ferro-chrome, which is primarily used in the production of stainless steel, where it is an essential and non-substitutable input.

Consolidated's third production centre, held through its wholly-owned subsidiary Consolidated Nickel, is near Kambalda in the WA Goldfields

Right: Processing Plant at Woodie Woodie manganese mine.
Below: Drill rig exploring Pilbara tenement area.

- one of the world's premier nickel provinces. The company holds the Beta Hunt nickel mine and the adjacent East Alpha development project.

The combined resource base of this large underground mining complex is 2.1 million tonnes at 3.6 percent nickel for 74,000 contained nickel tonnes.

The Beta Hunt mine currently produces 5,000 nickel tonnes per annum, with ore delivered to BHP Billiton's nickel concentrator in Kambalda some five kilometres from the operation. Ore production has been underway since November 2003.

The nearby East Alpha Project is being developed as a second nickel operation and will increase production from the complex to between 9,000 and 10,000 tonnes per annum in 2006. Nickel, like chromite, is a key ingredient in the manufacture of stainless steel.

While Consolidated's growth to date has been driven by the success of its steel-related mineral businesses, the company's next growth platform is based on the development of new commodity areas such as zinc and copper. Both are also influenced by strong demand from China's growing middle class.

The company has committed to a strategic 33 percent investment in and partnership with ASX-listed mining group, Jabiru Metals, which is developing the high-grade Jaguar zinc-copper project near the historic Teutonic Bore base metals mine around Leonora in WA's Northeastern Goldfields.

Consolidated's directors hold the view the benefits of the company should be shared, in part, to the wider community, especially in areas with relevance to the mining industry. Consolidated has established several

initiatives to support community interests including major donations to the Leukaemia Foundation, the Royal Flying Doctor Service, St Vincent de Paul, the Asian Tsunami Appeal, Princess Margaret Hospital, the Balya Cancer Retreat and the Sir Norman Brearly Trust.

Consolidated is also committed to the education of future mining professionals through the provision of two educational scholarships, one with the Australasian Institute of Mining and Metallurgy and one with the WA School of Mines.

Bottom: Airleg miner operating at the Kambalda nickel mine.
Below: Shipping Manganese Ore out of Port Hedland.

MITSUI IRON ORE DEVELOPMENT

Mitsui Iron Ore Development is maximising opportunities for clients in a booming economy.

Western Australia is reaping the benefits of a world-wide boom in the resource industry.

The state is making the most of its great reserves of natural resources, feeding the growing appetite of world and in particular Asian markets.

A WA company which is working hard to meet the huge demand while maximising opportunities for clients is the Mitsui Iron Ore Development.

MIOD has been closely involved with the West Australian economy since its incorporation in 1970.

The company is a subsidiary of Mitsui & Co Japan, an organisation boasting a long association with Australia. It first established offices in Sydney in 1909.

Mitsui & Co Japan is a general trading company or "Sogo Shosha", commissioned to source raw materials for the rapidly expanding Japanese industry in the 1960s. It has grown from a simple trading company into a general business creator as the business model of Sogo Shosha transformed to accommodate the ever changing world economy structure.

Focusing on raw materials, MIOD originally opened its office in Melbourne before moving to Perth in 1975. It is now based in the heart of WA's capital, in the Exchange Plaza Building.

"Our goal in relocating to Perth was to actively manage investments which are centred on the resources sector of the state," MIOD general manager administration John Smith said.

The company has had a rich history of developing some of the biggest projects seen in Western Australia.

The Robe River Iron Associates Joint Venture was launched in 1970 on the basis of the biggest initial iron ore sales contract in the world.

MIOD has been involved in the endeavour ever since and holds – through various companies and partnerships – 33 percent of the project.

In recent years, the company has been assisting the consolidation and expansion of its many Joint Ventures.

In 2002 a new mine was established at West Angelas, 110km west of Newman.

From there Robe transports iron by rail 330km to the North-West port of Cape Lambert for export to Japan, China, Korea, Taiwan and Europe.

In 1990 MIOD established a wholly owned subsidiary company, Mitsui Iron Ore Corporation and acquired a 7 percent share in the original Goldsworthy Mining Operation, the first iron ore miner in the Pilbara region.

Two years later, MIOC commenced shipments from the Yandi Joint Venture (7 percent owned) and in 2002 production commenced at Mining Area C. BHPBilliton Iron Ore is the majority owner and manager of MIOC's Joint Ventures.

Mitsui Iron Ore Development has been a major active participant in the development of the iron ore industry in Western Australia.

Below: Robe River Operations, Cape Lambert.

But it has not all been smooth sailing in the resources industry. There have been some tough times too.

"In the 1960s and 70s, the iron ore industry experienced low productivity levels, industrial unrest, oil crises, economic depression, major mine accidents, cyclones, poor communications and a harsh operating environment," Mr Smith said.

"But MIOD remained an investor and encouraged the use of the latest technology to overcome the inherent disadvantages of remote locations and in some instances inferior quality products.

"We are proud that despite the early problems in the industry, iron ore has emerged as a major industry, employer and exporter for Western Australia."

MIOD continues to assist the Joint Venture operators to improve efficiency so the investments maintain their positions as the most cost effective operations in the world.

But the company is also serious about playing an active part in the community it has helped to build.

MIOD is involved with community initiatives including the Australia-Japan Society, Constable Care Project, Multicultural Harmony Week and the Pannawonica Rodeo.

In addition, capital projects including Balya Cancer Retreat and Cossack Cemetery refurbishment have received financial assistance from MIOD.

MIOD has helped Western Australia grow in many ways over the past 36 years. And the company is upbeat about its future endeavours in the booming state.

Staff from left to right: (back row) Alison Hall, Elissa D'Onofrio, Stephanie Tomsic, Phebe Pan and Tom Okubo. (front row) Jun Konno, Paul Sukagawa and John Smith. Above: MIOD office in Exchange Plaza.

BGC (AUSTRALIA) PTY LTD

Business legend Len Buckeridge has been helping West Australians build their "Great Australian Dream" for more than four decades.

The pioneer of Western Australia's building industry, Len Buckeridge, strongly believes every Australian has a right to own his own home.

Mr Buckeridge has been helping West Australians reach that dream since the 1960s when, as a newly qualified architect, he first identified a need for low-cost but high-quality housing in the growing state.

Since then he has gone from humble, self-funded beginnings to become the owner of one of WA's biggest private company groups – BGC.

Along the way, the home-grown businessman has made many friends and more than a fair share of detractors. His progressive methods often challenged inflexible authorities and stubborn unions, as Mr Buckeridge recalled in a rare interview at a *WA Business News* Success and Leadership Breakfast.

Below: BGC Centre, Perth CBD.

"I did a house in Fremantle Road in Gosnells. It had a 75mm concrete slab on the floor and the council said 'no, you can't build that because it has a concrete floor ... the lady at the house would get sore legs walking on the concrete'," Mr Buckeridge remembered.

"Eventually I thought 'stuff you'. We built it. I don't think we ever got a building licence for it ... but it was built (with the concrete floor). I think it would be fair to say now about 90 percent of houses have concrete floors."

Mr Buckeridge started in the construction trade in 1961, making a name for himself building thousands of flats around Perth.

"If you think back to 1959, (there were) the little old ladies with the enclosed sleep-outs and families living on the side of them because there was a desperate house shortage," Mr Buckeridge said.

"My view was that flats were preferable to the enclosed sleep-out. Also at that same time we had cattle boat loads of migrants spilling into the country and no one would make provision of housing, so it was just an endless rush. I think in one year we built 1,200 units, which at that time was a very large number."

Taking control of the failing company Comfort Homes in 1974, he made his move into the single-residential building market, forming Dalfield Homes in 1976.

In 1980 Mr Buckeridge worked on expanding his interests in the market and formed various partnerships with other home building companies such as Les Friday Homes, National Homes and statesman Homes. Since then, similar companies have also been established in the BGC group which recently took full ownership of J-Corp.

It was during this period of expansion in the home building industry that the need for continuity of material supplies and fittings became obvious. This led Mr Buckeridge to focus on developing product supply companies. Roof tile plants, plumbing product companies, concrete plants and similar ventures were established under the BGC banner from 1984.

But there was another reason why Mr Buckeridge wanted to supply his own materials.

"(In) the 60s, the building unions had a good method of stopping construction," Mr Buckeridge said. "They'd stop concrete pours in the middle of them, so I thought, 'you bastards I'll fix you'. So I got into the concrete business.

"Unions then went to the cement companies and said 'if you supply that fellow, we will shut you down'. There were two cement producers, Swan and Cockburn and they wouldn't supply cement. So I said to them 'well, if you don't, I will make my own', and they had a bit of a giggle about that. So one year later, I was making cement."

By expanding its services, BGC broadened its base and insulated itself from fluctuations in the building market. Another sign of business vision was the group's diversification and investment in contracting, leading to the purchase of General Bulldozing in 1993. This proved a highly successful acquisition. The end result was the creation of the thriving BGC Contracting division that has grown to produce a hundred-fold its original annual turnover.

BGC also includes a flourishing commercial and unit building division which has received industry accolades and distinctions. It was awarded the 2005 MBA Excellence in Construction Award for the Canning Vale College, the Boronia Pre-Release Centre for Women and the University of Western Australia's Molecular and Chemical Science Building.

Several city properties have also been built by the company, including its impressive 20-storey BGC Centre in the heart of Perth.

BGC has also contributed to the development and growth of bustling land developments in Alexander Heights, Palm Lakes and Caversham.

The company turns over more than $1.4 billion a year and has more than 20 operating divisions with 3,500 staff and 3,000 subcontractors. Its operations extend to all of Australia's mainland states and internationally into East Asia and New Zealand.

More than three quarters of the homes built in Western Australia each year contain some BGC product, from the BGC Residential brand, such as National, Commodore or Impressions, to the group's materials such as roof tiling, windows, insulation or blokpave.

Government tenders for public housing and works continue to be awarded to the group as the lowest bidder, which highlights not only BGC's capabilities in the construction industry but also its commitment to savings. These are effectively passed onto the tax payers, many of whom are aspiring to their own dreams of home ownership.

Mr Buckeridge, who was recognised with the James Hardie Architectural Prize in 1960 and more recently named the Ernst and Young Master Entrepreneur of the Year for 2003, said home ownership was the right of every Australian and a sign of a healthy society.

"I think people living on a bit of territory, on their own little kingdom, in the impersonal world, it really makes the man. You know the bloke can go home, build a boat in his backyard, or plant a garden, or the kids can play in the backyard," Mr Buckeridge said.

"I think housing is a very important social issue (but) it is being neglected and it can only get worse. If you live in Sydney it is an impossible dream. What's happened is the true believers have become the forgotten people and there is no doubt the lower income workers are just screwed out of housing, it's just terrible."

Mr Buckeridge's strong principals and business foresight over the past four decades have shaped the success of BGC and helped generations of West Aussies build their own homes.

MARKETFORCE

Marketforce may be Western Australia's oldest advertising and marketing agency but it has never had trouble coming up with new and fresh ideas.

The innovative company was ranked in the top three creative agencies in Australia in 2005 and, the same year, WA marketing magazine *Campaign Brief* wrote: "In the 21 years of *Campaign Brief*, never has one agency been so far in front of the field."

Marketforce chairman John Driscoll believes those accolades are testament to the fact the agency's founding philosophy is as relevant now as it was in 1974.

The agency has a passionate belief that WA can produce the best work and the best results in any field – with advertising no different.

Marketforce formed in 1974 from the merger of iconic ad agencies Warnock Sandford Williams (formerly AJ Williams, WA's first advertising agency) and Bean Birrell.

More than 100 employees are based in its West Perth offices.

Many successful and high-profile organisations trust Marketforce to help promote their brands or ideals. The agency has handled campaigns for Lotterywest, Peters and Brownes, SGIO and D'Orsogna. It also developed the Office of Road Safety's latest award-winning commercial "Dave", which aims to educate drivers as to the dangers of speed.

Mr Driscoll said the firm was proud of its reputation for integrity and honesty in dealings with clients and suppliers and it had been rewarded with some of the longest client partnerships in the industry.

The agency has also been the primary supplier of advertising media services to successive state governments, regardless of their political persuasion.

"Our innovative and entrepreneurial attributes are two of the reasons many companies seek us out," Mr Driscoll said.

An example of this was Marketforce's involvement in the 1987 America's Cup.

When Australia II won the 1983 America's Cup, Marketforce's then chairman, Colin Mullins, immediately sent an executive to Newport to document every facet of the event and then developed a plan for successfully holding the America's Cup in WA. This initiative ensured Marketforce was the number one choice to be the Royal Perth Yacht Club's exclusive marketing partner for the 1987 event in WA.

The agency is also community-minded, willing to put back into the industry and the community.

In 2005, the state government announced it would spend up to $1 million on a public education campaign to fight the spread of cane toads in WA. Many agencies lobbied for the lucrative advertising account but the Marketforce board agreed the cane toad represented the greatest single environmental threat to WA in modern times and the agency should do the work at no charge.

Marketforce became a sponsor of *WA Business News*' 40Under40 awards in 2005, to ensure the marketing and advertising industry was recognised. It also makes a conscious commitment to provide a taste of advertising to as many work experience people as possible.

Marketforce's vision is to be the best in its field in every endeavour and the company aims to bring new opportunities to its business through innovation and technology while remaining steadfastly committed to the value of a brand.

Below: Marketforce reception.

PROFILES IN EXCELLENCE

1975 – 2005

YEAR EST.	COMPANY NAME	PAGE
1975	EBM Insurance Brokers	174
1978	Horwath Chartered Accountants	176
1983	Dôme Coffees Australia Pty Ltd	178
1984	Edge Employment Solutions	180
1984	JMG	182
1985	Asgard Wealth Solutions	184
1985	Burswood Entertainment Complex	186
1985	Technology Precinct	226
1986	GRD Limited	188
1987	ComputerCORP	190
1988	Humfrey Land Developments	192
1989	AOT Consulting	194
1989	Hydramet Australia	196
1992	Action Mining Services	198
1992	Creating Communities	202
1993	Alliance Recruitment	236
1993	WA Business News	204
1994	Town of Victoria Park	206
1994	Westnet	208
1996	Water Corporation	210
2000	Forest Products Commission	237
2001	Sally Malay Mining Limited	214
2001	WA Local Government Association	216
2002	Armadale Redevelopment Authority	218
2002	Calibre Projects	220
2002	Lease Equity	222
2003	Department of Industry and Resources	224
2004	Azure Captial	230
2004	Mitsui E&P Australia Pty Ltd	232
2004	Perth Convention Exhibition Centre	234
2005	Antenna Business Development Agency	183

EBM INSURANCE BROKERS

EBM's success story based on professionalism and commitment to clients needs.

Elkington Bishop Molineaux Insurance Brokers Pty Ltd (EBM) has been the stand out success story of Australia's insurance broking industry during the last three decades. What started in Perth as a two-man operation in 1975 has grown into Australia's largest privately-owned insurance broking firm, with headquarters in Perth and significant offices in Melbourne, Sydney, Brisbane Gold Coast, Kalgoorlie, Geraldton, Bunbury and Margaret River.

The road from minnow to one of the country's industry leaders has not always been easy, but its solid foundations ensured that EBM's clients always had access to advice and products that suited their businesses perfectly and at competitive prices. It is a formula that is still used by EBM today – the right advice with the right product at the right price.

The foundations were laid in 1975 when the firm's founders, Neville Elkington and Alan Bishop, left their senior positions in a big international broking house to start EBM. They realised that they could provide a more personal, professional and prompt service to the insuring public than the international firms – and they had the experience and expertise to offer their new clients professional advice and products to exactly match their needs.

The founders' culture of providing excellent service is still the cornerstone of EBM's continuing growth and this commitment to client needs is foremost in the firm's modus operandi. It is a culture that is passed on to all staff members, who now total more than 130 dedicated people.

EBM's growth path has been spectacular. Annual turnover now exceeds $100,000,000 from a base that includes more than 90,000 clients ranging from individuals to large national corporations. EBM is one of the few brokers in Australia that can offer a complete range of insurance products and solutions to such a broad range of clients.

Most of EBM's growth to industry leader has been through a combination of targeted business acquisitions, organic growth and by word-of-mouth endorsement of its personal service and staff expertise.

EBM's Managing Director of 20 years, Jeff Adams, said the firm's success could be attributed to its total commitment to clients.

"The key has been to stay focused on providing excellent personal, professional and prompt service," Mr Adams said.

"We have done this by structuring the company into small, dynamic units in specific areas within corporate, commercial, regional, mining, professional and personal market sectors. Each unit has dedicated and qualified staff empowered to service their select group of clients."

This approach has enabled EBM to make major inroads into many market sectors in which it has established specialist insurance programs and products.

This has led to the opening of its satellite offices. For example, the Kalgoorlie office resulted from EBM's involvement in the mining and the mining services industries. EBM's eastern states offices were created to service its national accounts and provide corporate clients with personal service.

Product innovation is a key ingredient to EBM's success. This has resulted in the development of programs to suit various trade associations such as plumbers, painters, butchers, builders, cleaners, general trades' people and labour hire organisations.

EBM has also focused on the real estate industry, fishing and pearling, mining and property management. For individuals, there is RentCover for landlords, StudentCover for school children, EquineCover for horse lovers and a host of other tailored market segments.

Below: (standing) Terry O'Connor QC AM, Dalton Gooding and Michael Monaghan AM, (seated) John O'Dea, Alan Bishop, Jeff Adams and Ian Goddard.

Above: At EBM, we pride ourselves on our friendly and professional service.

The internet created opportunities for further innovation in the insurance broking industry and EBM became the first (and possibly only broker in Australia so far) to offer individual personal accident cover for students online. This service provides parents with peace-of-mind protection at a low cost and has created a pipeline for a range of other innovative web-based products.

EBM Chairman and Joint Managing Director, Alan Bishop, said the road to success over three decades had been paved with hard work to overcome many obstacles.

"These have been due, in part, to the fickle nature of the insurance market and to its contraction over most of those years," Mr Bishop said. "The problems in the insurance industry were coupled with an increasingly tough legislative and compliance regime.

"EBM has emerged the stronger for it and is well positioned to continue its original mission of providing personal, professional and prompt service.

"It will do so by using its unique system of small, dynamic business units operating within a large support system with international connections."

While EBM is focused on customer service, it is also committed to ensuring the insurance broking industry reaches the highest-possible standards of professionalism.

In 1982, EBM became a foundation member of the National Insurance Brokers Association of Australia (NIBA), and has been actively involved in association endeavours to lift industry standards since then.

The company received NIBA's prestigious award for Business Excellence in 1987-88. In 1996 Alan Bishop was elected national president of NIBA – a position he held for two years. In 2004, he was awarded the Lex McKeown Trophy and became an Honorary Fellow of NIBA – a title shared by only six others. He has also been active in NIBA's WA chapter and served in a number of positions, including state chairman.

EBM has also been active in international insurance markets, including representation at Lloyds of London. In 1999, EBM assisted in the founding of the Asia Australasia Alliance, an international network of insurance brokers throughout South-East Asia, China, New Zealand and the Pacific Islands.

EBM's Board includes two directors with strong connections to the West Coast Eagles Football Club – the club's Chairman, Dalton Gooding, and past chairman, Terry O'Connor QC AM, who is also a former commissioner of the Australian Football League.

Michael Monaghan AM, a respected Western Australian businessman, has been on the EBM Board since 1984. Mr Monaghan is a former president of the Australian and West Australian Hotels and Hospitality Associations and a member of the Western Australian Tourism Commission, EventsCorp Committee, Liquor Industries Council and the Liquor Industry Road Safety Council.

EBM's commitment to professionalism in the industry is reflected in its focus on staff training and development, both within its own ranks and through the industry association. Mr Bishop was the prime mover in establishing the recently-created insurance cadet system, which encourages young people to consider making insurance their chosen career. EBM has trained and employed many of these cadets since the program's inception in 2003.

All EBM staff members are involved in continuous training programs and are required to maintain a high standard of expertise in their field. Some 57 EBM staff hold Diplomas in Financial Services for Insurance Broking.

For several years, EBM has also been a proud sponsor and supporter of United Way and Teen Challenge – part of its commitment to the community as a good corporate citizen.

HORWATH CHARTERED ACCOUNTANTS

Horwath offers a local, independent accounting and business advice service, backed by its national and international network.

Expert and timely advice is crucial in today's fast paced business environment. And these highly sought qualities are synonymous with accounting firm Horwath.

The company is one of Australia's leading associations of independent accounting, tax and business consulting firms. The firm provides services that are highly tuned into the local business environment.

Horwath has been part of the West Australian community for nearly 30 years. Since opening its doors as Ansell, Price and Atkins in 1978, through its years as Duesburys, and since joining the Horwath international network in 1997, the firm has been providing expert advice and assistance to business and private clients locally, nationally and internationally.

It was originally based in Perth's Murray Street, then 'Duesburys House' in Ord Street, West Perth, before moving to its present location at 128 Hay Street, Subiaco in 1998.

Horwath clients benefit from the firm's membership of one of the largest global accounting networks and its affiliated offices in all major Australian financial centres.

In addition to professional services in a wide cross section of industries and professions, Horwath is a leading adviser to medical specialists, motor dealers, owners and managers of family businesses and all levels of participants in the oil, gas and resources sectors.

The firm specialises in the delivery of financial services and products to its clients, including internal control and performance reviews, valuations and assistance with budgetary and finance funding applications, mergers and acquisitions, and capital raisings.

Horwath also provides a full range of traditional accounting, tax and assurance services.

The Perth office is particularly proud of its longstanding support of the not-for-profit sector.

Horwath's culture is reflected in the way its offices work together to help clients and develop staff. This is illustrated by the organisation's values, summed up by the acronym 'REACH' – Respect, Recognition and Reward;

Right: The Horwath offices at 128 Hay Street, Subiaco have a welcome feel for clients and visitors.

Opposite page: Horwath directors (clockwise from top left); Glyn O'Brien, David Stevens, Russell Garvey, Peter Moltoni, Mauri Mucciacciaro and Tony Bevan.

Bottom: Horwath is one of the largest global accounting and business advisory networks.

Encouraging teamwork; Achievement of excellence; Celebrating success and working hard; all of which represent Horwath.

"The firm works closely with clients to gain a full understanding of their business and personal objectives," Perth managing director David Stevens said.

"With a focus on developing long-term relationships, we use our experience and skills to offer proactive and relevant service and advice in order to help our clients."

Prominent industry knowledge and accreditations of its directors and staff have enabled Horwath to meet the growing desire among clients for stable, personalised service, with an appropriate focus on the traditional compliance services they need and the specialised services they want.

With increased competition in the accountancy sector, Horwath continues to work hard to ensure the firm's clients achieve their goals and improve their wealth and assurance.

The aim is always to exceed their clients' expectations.

DÔME COFFEES AUSTRALIA PTY LTD

Developing from a small, specialist coffee roaster, Dôme Coffees Australia Pty Ltd has grown to a multi-million dollar international enterprise while remaining true to its core focus of producing the world's finest coffees.

At any time of the day, the coffee machine at Dôme Coffees Australia's café support centre is not only extracting the world's finest coffees, but also great conversation and creative ideas.

Staff make their own favourites and discuss business in a section of the Nedlands building decorated like one of Dôme's European-style cafés.

Fitting that at a company priding itself on producing the world's finest coffees, many decisions are made around the coffee machine.

Chief executive Nigel Oakey says it provides informal opportunities for staff to raise ideas and make decisions, whether it is support staff, or café managers and café team members popping in for training or a catch-up with their operations leader.

The relaxed nature of the office belies its ambitious outlook but is part of Mr Oakey's style of doing business.

"I aim to remove the 'politicking' and make everyone part of the decision-making process where possible," he said.

"I don't want us to build an empire with a traditionally large, bureaucratic headquarters. Our aim is to keep the number of people "off-stage" few in number and highly productive and swell the number of people in front of the customers."

Mr Oakey said the company used a metaphor to describe its way of doing business, with a vision to create The Greatest Coffee Show on Earth.

"We call the business a show and the cafés the stages," he explained.

"Employees are actors – either those off-stage (head office), back stage (café kitchens), or on stage (out the front of the café) and the customers are the guests of the show.

"The actors have a script to follow (the business processes) but how they play their parts is all-important.

"If they do well, then everyone else cheers them on."

Mr Oakey said reliability was an important factor of Dôme Coffees' success.

"Customers should be able to visit any Dôme café and always receive the same high-quality coffee and meal," he said.

Dôme Coffees Australia was created in 1989, when Patria Jafferies joined Phil May, who had been hand-roasting beans, operating Western Roast Coffee since 1983.

Dôme Coffees Australia was established to import and roast the world's finest coffees and the pair opened the first Dôme café in Cottesloe in November 1990. In 1993, they established the Dôme franchise network and went international later that year, opening two cafés as a joint venture in Singapore.

On December 10, 2003, Dôme Coffees Australia Pty Ltd was acquired via management buy-out with Navis Capital Partners (Asia) Ltd.

Dôme now has more than 80 outlets in seven countries – Australia, Malaysia, Singapore, Indonesia, UAE, Philippines and Brunei, with more on the horizon, including Bahrain and Qatar.

Within the group's brand stable is also a growing chain of espresso and panini bars called "Cino to Go".

Mr Oakey said Dôme's original owners and the franchisees had taken the brand to the public but the business had changed since he joined the team

as chief executive in 2001. He said the company was set up to produce and sell great blends of coffee.

"It was the manufacturer of a physical product," Mr Oakey said. "Now we are a retailer selling an experience."

Mr Oakey said through national and international expansion they had doubled the size of the company since 2001.

However, Dôme also consolidated, buying back many of the franchised cafés in the metropolitan area.

"We believe that if we are a café owner ourselves we can run the company with more integrity and can relate to other franchisees' issues," Mr Oakey said.

"We try new products or services at our cafés first and franchisees are happy when they become involved because they know they are incorporating something that has been tested properly."

Mr Oakey said Dôme cafés had three points of difference from other coffee chains.

"Our cafés have a European ambience with quality interiors, we have great-tasting, good-value food and table service," he said.

"Our main competitors are independent cafés rather than other coffee chains."

Mr Oakey said the rapid growth of the specialty coffee market in many economies around the world encouraged Dôme's strategies of expansion.

He attributed much of that growth to individuals' increasing understanding of coffee – with the rise in purchases of plungers and home espresso machines.

"With more awareness of the alternative to instant coffee more people seek that," he said.

"They will visit cafés on the weekends or go out for a takeaway coffee during work rather than having a cup of instant in the office," he said.

Mr Oakey said one of the hallmarks of Dôme Coffee's success was the adage "think global act local".

"We have a brand and as long as the core stays true we can make it relevant to countries it operates in," he said.

"We have a certain level of standards at all cafés but we can adapt 30 percent of our menu to local market requirements or translate menus to the local language."

Dôme Coffee Australia's five-year plan is reasonably aggressive and global but sustainable, says Mr Oakey.

"We'll not grow for the sake of growth," he said. "Our focus is on conducting business the best way possible – whether that's embracing new technology, changing our menus or providing new opportunities to successful franchisees.

"Everything is focused on shareholder value, created by staff and guest satisfaction producing the Greatest Coffee Show on Earth!"

Above: The warmth and intimacy of one of Dôme Coffees Australia's most recent European-style cafes.

Below: A selection of Dôme's most popular coffees.

Opposite page: The crema, the true essence of perfect coffee.

EDGE EMPLOYMENT SOLUTIONS

EDGE Employment Solutions was established in Perth in 1984 based on Dr Greg Lewis' Masters thesis on finding new avenues to open employment for people with disabilities.

Dr Greg Lewis's research demonstrated that people with disabilities, when provided with the right on-the-job training and support, were capable of open employment – a view not shared throughout the general community, especially the business community, at that point in time.

It was the view of EDGE that, given opportunities, people with disabilities could perform at the same levels of speed and productivity expected of other workers in a company.

This research formed the basis for EDGE, which now employees 60 staff at its Hood Street premises in Subiaco, overseen by managing director Sue Robertson.

From the outset, EDGE's vision was to enable people with disabilities to establish careers in open employment that are of mutual benefit to the employee, employer and the community.

Bringing this vision to fruition has not always been smooth sailing, with EDGE having to overcome its fair share of obstacles to find success.

EDGE was established at a time when the general unemployment level was well over 10 percent, with youth unemployment over 20 percent.

Given that EDGE's primary focus was within the youth market, it was clear that funding would be needed and EDGE would need to establish a position within WA's corporate sector for its vision to become a reality.

In its early years, EDGE struggled to secure government funding, as its focus on open employment did not meet the funding guidelines of the Handicapped Persons Assistance Act at that point in time. It was only after this act was repealed, and the Disability Services Act was implemented in 1986, that funding was secured and EDGE could move forward with confidence that its vision and mission could be achieved.

For EDGE to create a profile within the corporate business world, it was essential the company presented itself as a business, not a welfare agency. The appointment of a high profile corporate board went a long way towards securing the appropriate image.

A corporate image, coupled with the guarantee of post-placement support and back-up, helped EDGE to secure important early commitments from companies such as Coles and Wesfarmers. The company's partnership with Coles resulted in 250 jobs for people with disabilities, while its association with Wesfarmers resulted in 35 jobs, primarily in Bunnings' stores. This partnership was profiled at an International Labour Organisation Conference.

EDGE has also pioneered many initiatives and programs, including establishing partnerships with big business and the public sector, keynote addresses at international conferences around the world and publications in international journals on employment for people with disabilities; supporting athletes with disabilities to balance their training, work and study demands in the lead up to the Sydney and Athens Paralympics; development of an icon building in Subiaco, which demonstrates that commercial development can accommodate people with disabilities without compromising function, design or cost; establishing partnerships around Australia between disability employment agencies and group training organisations, resulting in several hundred people with disabilities undertaking apprenticeships; and delivering net savings to the taxpayer of $15 million in unpaid pensions and subsidies over the past 20 years.

As well as raising community awareness, it is the savings to the taxpayer that completes EDGE's vision of providing a service that is of mutual benefit to the employee, employer and the wider community.

In fact, it is a vision that has been contagious within the WA community and the broader Australian workplace. When EDGE was established in 1984, it was the only employment agency in this field in Australia; now there are more than 300 such agencies around Australia.

What is also obvious to the people of EDGE is the difference they have made to the attitudes of the WA public. The increased recognition amongst the business community that people with disabilities are a valuable labour resource and that addressing the issues faced by people who are economically disadvantaged makes good business sense, as well as being good for society, has much to do with EDGE's continued good work.

With such positive results already achieved, the future for EDGE looks bright and the people of WA can be proud that an agency of EDGE's calibre and reputation is in their corner when helping people with disabilities find work.

Below: Baulderstone Clough employee Ian Newman monitoring traffic in the Northbridge Tunnel.

Milestones in the company's history include:

*Above: EDGE's recently completed head-
quarters in Subiaco, built to the highest
standards for physical access.
Left: Managing director, Sue Robertson.*

September 1983	Completion of research underpinning Project Employment;
February 1984	Establishment of Project Employment;
August 1984	Incorporation of Project Employment;
1986 – 1988	Establishment of National Network of Project Employment services in Bunbury, Adelaide, Tweed Heads, Darwin, Albury and Wollongong;
September 1986	Procurement of commonwealth government funding;
1987	Winner of the Association for the Scientific Study of Intellectual Disability National Research Prize;
June 1991	1,000 jobs secured for people with disabilities, who would normally be in receipt of the disability support pension;
January 1999	2,000 jobs secured for people with disabilities;
July 1999	Assisted to establish disability employment service in Indonesia;
September 2003	3,000 jobs secured for people with disabilities;
July 2005	3,456 jobs secured for people with disabilities;
September 2005	Assisted in establishment of a disability employment service in Singapore.

JMG

JMG has worked successfully with many leading brands since its establishment in 1984.

Below: Just part of the JMG team.

The JMG team of senior, experienced and proven professionals has contributed to the growth and success of many renowned companies including Challenge Bank, Ikea, RAC, BankWest, Australia Post and more recently StateWest Credit Society.

As one of Western Australia's longest established marketing and advertising companies, JMG developed a reputation in the 80s and 90s as a leading below-the-line specialist. JMG has evolved over the years to meet the changing needs of business while reflecting improvements and advances in thinking, innovation and technology. The JMG of today has fourteen full-time employees and will turnover around $5 million in 2005/06. As a dynamic, full-service marketing communications company, JMG has a structure designed to complement the requirements of clients seeking growth through innovative marketing and creativity. Skills in database marketing and one-to-one communication teamed with the ability to exploit technological advances allow JMG to bring a new perspective to strategic planning to all of its clients.

The central philosophy around which JMG operates is to treat each client's business as if it were their own. JMG seeks to form true client partnerships through collaboration based on trust, honesty, transparency, accountability and commitment.

"While branding is the key element in any company's arsenal, JMG ensures that clients embrace a broader perspective in the marketing mix to engage and win the friendship of customers," said JMG executive director Paul McDowell.

"With the continued fragmentation of broadcast media, the creative concept must now be able to not only work in media but also in electronic and telephony communications."

"As JMG strives forward, we are always searching for new solutions to capture the attention of new customers. This has never been more evident in the sense that traditional media has been upstaged. Traditional media is becoming increasingly less effective in communicating to 16-to-24 year olds who, by the use of technology, can determine what they want to watch when they want to watch it. We must now talk to demographic groups in their own vernacular and on their own turf."

From the days when JMG founder Jim Murphy continually preached that one-to-one communication was an integral part of marketing and growth strategies, there has always been a strong emphasis in all JMG campaigns to put the customer first.

"An example of this is our client StateWest Credit Society. This organisation constantly receives accolades from their customer-base for the very personal approach they have to marketing and customer relations. The customer really does feel special when they are personally recognised and treated as a member - not just a number. By understanding what drives this approach, we are able to ensure key brand messages penetrate through all levels of a particular organisation – ultimately allowing us to speak directly with that organisation's customers," said Mr McDowell.

"Research consistently shows that word-of-mouth is the single biggest source of new business – far outstripping all other forms of advertising, marketing and promotion,"

Recognising and instigating strategies that reflect this and other significant research outcomes is key to JMG's longevity in the Western Australian marketplace.

ANTENNA BUSINESS DEVELOPMENT AGENCY

Established in May 2005, this unique new West Australian business was created to assist clients to increase sales volumes, raise market share and improve customer profitability.

Formerly a business unit within JMG Marketing offering call centre and data collection services, Antenna has evolved into a state-of-the-art business development agency offering services well beyond telemarketing. Specialising in database development, gathering market intelligence, outbound telephone and electronic direct marketing and CRM campaigns, Antenna has emerged as a specialist provider of business development services.

The concept for the provision of specialist business development services arose from the identification of a niche opportunity to provide marketing support to sales and business development managers. The concept was researched internationally and a suite of services and products developed to provide customers with an end-to-end business development process.

The business development process developed by Antenna revolves around the development of customer and prospect databases and the creation of innovative sales driven marketing techniques including lead generation, appointment setting, electronic marketing and CRM programs that assist companies to increase sales volumes, capture market share and improve the lifetime value of customers.

Antenna assists both developing and mature organisations to identify and engage new and existing markets. Through the business development process, clients gain a better understanding of customer and competitor markets and be provided with business development programs that stimulate demand and create sales pipelines. This ensures that a direct return on sales and marketing expenditure can be generated.

The Antenna icon is a brand device representing the transmitting and receiving of frequency messaging. Similarly, Antenna Business Development Agency is a channel utilised to transmit critical messages and information between potential customers and Antenna's clients.

Antenna's young and dynamic teams provide clients with a positive integration of skills and expertise. A clever combination of traditional sales and marketing disciplines plus technological innovations means this tight-knit management team works as an integrated unit focusing on delivering measurable business growth to Antenna's clients.

Since launching, Antenna has established an array of clients encompassing leading brands such as Bluescope Steel, Bunnings, ComputerCorp, Automasters, and StateWest Credit Society. The attraction of these clients represents successful milestones in the evolution of the company, particularly being given the privilege of working alongside Telstra as one of only three agencies nationally to oversee and develop broadband sales executions.

Antenna is still in its early stages of growth and the organisation envisions further development of a broad range of marketing methodologies with the ultimate aim of excelling in the field of business development. Antenna is in a unique position in the market, creating an escalating awareness of its sales-generated activities. Its efforts challenge traditional marketing thinking, to the point where business development will ultimately be synonymous with any business's marketing efforts.

A young and dynamic team focused on delivering measurable results to clients; (from left to right) Bartholomew Hart – managing director, Howie Hughes – group account director, Farah Shah – marketing executive, Creswell Casey – general manager – electronic marketing services.

ASGARD WEALTH SOLUTIONS

*The idea was simple;
create a company that
offers the resources and
support of financial
advisers, to financial
advisers.*

In 1985, Asgard Wealth Solutions, formerly known as Sealcorp, was the brainchild of a small group of financial planners who saw a gap in the market for a service that would give financial advisers the tools and support they needed to enhance the quality of advice they gave to clients, and better manage their practices.

It was one of the first companies established in Australia by financial planners for financial planners. Today, the company operates two complementary businesses – Asgard, which is one of Australia's largest and most awarded platforms, and the advice business solutions business of which the company's financial advisory dealer group, Securitor, is a part.

Over time, Asgard Wealth Solutions has gone from strength to strength and now employs 450 staff at their Perth office, located at Central Park, St Georges Terrace. The company employs 670 staff throughout Australia.

A major moment in the history of this company came to pass in 1988 with the launch of the Asgard platform through a superannuation product called the Asgard Independence Plan. Within four years FUA on the platform had grown to $1 billion and doubled again by 1994.

In 1997, St.George acquired the company, heralding a new phase in the company's development.

November 2005 saw the company change its corporate name from Sealcorp to Asgard Wealth Solutions, which was considered to be more reflective of the full spectrum of services offered by the company.

It's no wonder, with Asgard Wealth Solutions' forward thinking and creative approach to finance, that they celebrated their 20th year of operation by reaching $20 billion FUA.

Today, Asgard Wealth Solutions is national company controlling more than eight percent of the market and manages the country's fifth biggest platform with $25.5 billion FUA as at February 2006.

Throughout its history Asgard Wealth Solutions has not only been the foundation for success for others by supplying quality financial products and support, they have been an innovative company that took pride in forging into new territory through the creation of new initiatives and programs.

When the Asgard platform was launched to the market in 1988 it was one of the industry's first. Its ability to give financial advisers the specific tools and support they needed to give top quality advice to investors and more efficiently manage their practices had not been seen before. 20 years later, the success is testament to the foresight of the company's founders.

The other huge success story for the company has been adviserNET, Australia's leading online business solution for financial advisers. The product, which was first designed and built in Perth in 1996, was an industry trailblazer. adviserNET allowed financial advisers the ability to buy and sell assets for their clients online at a time when most people didn't have an email address.

Since its inception, adviserNET has won a raft of industry awards. Most recently in 2005, for the third year in a row, it was voted the industry's

*Below: (left to right) CEO Geoff Lloyd with
the company's Perth based director team:
David Clark – institutional business
services, Jane O'Halloran –
corporate and staff development and
Janice Gardner – finance.*

*Opposite page: (top) CEO Geoff Lloyd;
(bottom) foyer at Asgard's Perth
headquarters at Central Park,
St Georges Terrace.*

number one online service for financial advisers by Investment Trends, an independent research house.

In the past 21 years, Perth has grown into a capital city to rival any in Australia It now has a growing economy with an ideal infrastructure for business, a highly skilled workforce, booming property prices and a very attractive lifestyle.

WA offers enormous opportunities for a wealth management company such as Asgard Wealth Solutions to continue to grow.

Since the formation of the Australian Stock Exchange in 1987, WA financial services businesses, like Asgard Wealth Solutions, have been particularly entrepreneurial and forward thinking in their approach to operations in order to maintain their relevance on the national financial services scene.

Now a company with a national footprint, Asgard Wealth Solutions is proud that it had its inception in Perth. While Asgard Wealth Solutions, as a business-to-business company, may not be as well known as some WA counterparts, it continues to be one of the state's biggest employers in financial services. In fact, the company has one of the biggest IT departments in the state.

Asgard Wealth Solutions stands for advice, confidence and solutions. The company exists to efficiently and reliably enable financial advice for the benefit of advisers and investors. The company's vision is a world where people have the financial confidence to be inspired by their future. And in creating this world, Asgard Wealth Solutions aims to continue to grow their business and ensure a long and prosperous future.

BURSWOOD ENTERTAINMENT COMPLEX

Opposite page: (top to bottom) Burswood Entertainment Complex Burswood Casino – 24/7, non-stop action and excitement; and the award-winning Convention Centre. Below: With nine restaurants and six bars, Burswood has something to suit every taste; (bottom) Holiday Inn Burswood, one of Perth's newest purpose-built hotels.

In December 1985, two coins were tossed in the air while the people of Western Australia watched and waited in anticipation of what the future would bring.

As the coins hit the ground – heads, tails or odds – it was official, the Burswood Casino was open and an exciting new era had commenced in Western Australia's tourism and hospitality industry.

Today, more than 20 years on, Burswood is a fully-integrated entertainment complex and has become a household name, synonymous with entertainment, world-class facilities and luxury accommodation.

Its home on the banks of the Swan River is only minutes from the CBD and airports. Burswood boasts a 24-hour Casino, 413-room InterContintental hotel, 291-room Holiday Inn, nine restaurants, six bars, a nightclub, a convention centre and meeting rooms, a 2,300-seat theatre, a 20,000-seat indoor stadium, expansive gardens and a host of recreation facilities, including an 18-hole public golf course, day spa, retail outlets and riverside cycling trails.

Burswood welcomes more than 4.5 million visitors a year (on average, 12,500 people a day) and is acknowledged as one of Western Australia's most significant tourism export earners, receiving more than 200 industry accolades for excellence since the start of operations.

The combined 704 hotel-room capacity and variety of offerings on one site also make Burswood one of the most desirable conference and exhibition destinations in Australia.

Providing dynamic and diverse career opportunities for its almost 3,000-strong work-force, Burswood is WA's largest single-site private employer and contributes significantly to the state through government taxes and levies, associated payroll costs and ongoing investment in training and development.

Burswood's staff play a vital role in the achievement of the company's vision to create a world-class entertainment precinct and, as the face of WA's largest hospitality organisation, are renowned for their friendliness and customer service.

As one of Western Australia's leading entertainment destinations, Burswood is proud to play host to some of the world's greatest artists and productions, including Mamma Mia, We Will Rock You, Saturday Night Fever, Boy from Oz, U2, Red Hot Chili Peppers, Neil Diamond, Mark Knopfler, Blondie, Coldplay, Tom Jones, the St. Petersburg Ballet and the New York Dance Company, to name just a few.

Recognising the important role it plays in the community, Burswood is committed to the responsible delivery of its gaming operations and to making a positive and long-term difference through its community relations, sponsorships and employee-involvement initiatives.

Burswood supports a number of local charities through its Helping You to Help Others Programme. Variety WA, Youth Focus, Make-a-Wish Foundation and Ronald McDonald House Charities are some of the community partners assisted through the provision of facilities and resources.

Every year, Burswood's 200-strong army of chefs prepare more than 11,000 litres of soup for distribution to Perth's homeless shelters and hostels in partnership with Foodbank WA. Other contributions include support for CrimeStoppers, charity Movies by Burswood, Storm the Stage Youth Arts Project, and the donation of unclaimed winnings in the Casino to the Western Australian Gaming Community Trust.

Burswood is also committed to working with local industry to continue to attract and secure world-class events and tourism opportunities for Perth. A highlight on the annual calendar is the Hyundai Hopman Cup and Burswood is proud to continue an 18-year tradition of bringing the best of the world's tennis action to Perth.

Adding a new dimension to the precinct is the development of a luxury residential community adjacent to the Complex. With views across the Burswood Park Golf Course, city and river, The Peninsula development is a joint venture between Burswood and Mirvac Fini and will offer a diverse mix of contemporary residences and luxurious apartments for up to 3,000 residents.

In September 2004, Burswood was acquired by Publishing and Broadcasting Limited (PBL), one of Australia's largest and most diversified media and entertainment groups. With its core businesses of gaming and entertainment, television production and broadcasting, magazine publishing and distribution, and strategic investment in key digital media and entertainment businesses, PBL has identified significant opportunities to expand and improve every aspect of Burswood's business, demonstrating its commitment to both Burswood and Western Australia.

From the expansion of its international gaming operations through the construction of a new VIP international gaming facility, to an investment in upgrading and developing all food, beverage and entertainment offerings, Burswood is now positioned to move even faster towards reaching its goal of creating a world-class entertainment precinct.

The combined international marketing networks of PBL and the InterContinental Hotels Group promote Burswood and Western Australia in more overseas destinations than ever before, resulting in significant future growth and economic flow-on benefits for the state.

Burswood also understands the importance of remaining flexible and innovative to meet the changing needs and expectations of its customers, at both a local and international level. The need to continuously re-energise and re-invigorate its service offerings to reflect the changing face of Perth and Western Australia is paramount.

Building on its proud and spirited 20-year history of achievements, Burswood has embarked on an exciting journey of re-invention. By re-branding to Burswood Entertainment Complex in 2005, Burswood is sending a clear message to the world about what it offers ... and that's entertainment.

GRD LIMITED

Resource rich Western Australia is the perfect base for construction and development giant GRD Limited.

The company is the brainchild of its chairman Brettney Fogarty, who bought into various businesses, gradually building a strong enterprise hub that is now the GRD group.

The world industry leader is based in WA but its projects span the globe. The company's head office has always been in Perth, employing more than 1,000 people. But more than 460 of its staff work for GRD overseas and this number is growing.

Mr Fogarty said the company has a strong management team focused on project execution and delivering growth.

"The original mission of GRD, or UGM as it was initially known, was to become a resource engineering and development company," Mr Fogarty said.

"This mission has evolved to capitalise on the company's technical expertise through the opportunities in the waste market. GRD has now become a global construction and development company."

Its board members include executive chairman Mr Fogarty, former West Australian Premier the Hon. Richard Court AC, Steven Dean, Bruce Thomas and the company's secretary and executive director development Cliff Lawrenson. The management team also includes construction chief operating officer Malcolm Brown.

Since its beginning as the Union Gold Mining Company in 1986, the organisation has strived to achieve the best results for its shareholders while being an industry leader.

A year after its formation, the company listed on the stock exchange and in 1997 it acquired a 35 percent interest in Minproc.

One of its first major acquisitions was the 1998 purchase of the Macraes Mining Company with its main asset the Macraes Gold Project

in New Zealand. That same year, UGM changed its name to Gold and Resource Developments.

In 1999, the company commenced a major transformation with the acquisition and amalgamation of 100 percent of Minproc and the Macraes Mining Company.

GRD's most successful initiative is the development of the UR-3R technology which has resulted in the construction of the $75 million Eastern Creek Facility in Sydney, New South Wales, and the preferred contractor status for the delivery of Lancashire's waste strategy in the United Kingdom.

The $700 million Lancashire Waste Partnership PFI Project has a 25-year, $6 billion concession to process more than 20 million tonnes of waste for a population the size of Perth.

GRD's subsidiary Global Renewables has integrated a suite of the world's best commercially proven resource recovery technologies to create the Urban Resource — Reduction, Recovery and Recycling Process, which provides a truly sustainable solution to managing municipal solid waste.

GRD prides itself on the development of the UR-3R technology and being a world leader in mineral and waste-to-resource processing, especially nickel laterites, pressure leach and bio-digestion technologies.

And the company is expanding beyond the Australian shores, with growth hubs in South Africa, Brasil and the United Kingdom.

GRD has secured several major projects including BHP Billiton's $1.4 billion Ravensthorpe Nickel Project in Western Australia, CVRD's $1.6 billion Niquel do Vermelho Project in Brasil and the preferred contractor status for the delivery of Lancashire's waste strategy in the United Kingdom.

In 2005, GRD was admitted to the S&P/ASX 200 index on the Australian Stock Exchange, establishing itself as one of the country's prominent business organisations.

Right: The leach thickener and oxide flotation circuit at the Kansanshi Copper Project, Zambia.

Among the biggest challenges for GRD has been the cyclical nature of the engineering and mining industries. While WA is enjoying a booming economy, underpinned by a strong mining sector, the industry has not always fared as well. Good planning, foresight and expertise have ensured GRD has remained competitive and will continue to have a strong industry presence.

Another challenge has been the perception that GRD and GRD Minproc work only in the Australian gold industry. The company is now a global leader in nickel, gold and copper, with extensive experience throughout the world. It has also managed to successfully break into the UK waste market, one of the largest in the world.

GRD's expertise has seen it seize some great opportunities. For example, OceanaGold, which GRD listed on the stock exchange in 2004, possesses a difficult to develop ore body. It is through the technical expertise of OceanaGold and GRD Minproc, more specifically the specialist autoclave technology, that the ore body was successfully developed and the operations are continuing to expand.

The GRD group has made the most of the maturing resource sector and the internationalisation of Perth through the growing demand for resources, in particular from China.

The company is also very active in the community. The Fogarty Foundation encourages people to aim for excellence. It funds charitable programs that promote knowledge and ideas and creates opportunities for young people with goals and the potential to become leaders in the community.

Above: Eastern Creek UR-3R Facility, Sydney.

Left: Organic Growth Media (OGM) from the Eastern Creek UR-3R Facility.

The foundation, in partnership with GRD and the University of Western Australia, is funding undergraduate entry-level scholarships to foster the development of future business and community leaders in WA.

GRD's vision for the future is to become a truly global business in the construction and development industries with a strong presence in the waste to resource and mineral resource markets of the world.

COMPUTERCORP

ComputerCORP provides desktop management services, networks and products and advises customers on their IT strategies, implementing the most appropriate technology from a range of leading vendors. The company also manages elements of customer technology infrastructures to minimise costs and add value.

ComputerCORP was founded in Perth in 1987 with a mission to provide major Australian corporate, business, educational and government-based organisations with a stable, flexible, strategic IT business partner. It delivers goods and services throughout Australia, with city offices in Sydney, Adelaide, Canberra, Melbourne, Brisbane and Hobart and regional offices in Bunbury, Kalgoorlie and Launceston, complementing its Perth head office.

Despite more than 80 percent of the company's market being in the east coast states of Victoria, New South Wales and Queensland, ComputerCORP has not been tempted to leave WA.

Key management, infrastructure and resources are in WA and local business is also increasing, with a 10 percent growth from the 2003/2004 to 2004/2005 financial years.

The IT industry is a relatively young industry but is one of the world's fastest growing and companies in the industry have to diversify and adapt to satisfy customers' changing needs.

Strategic vision and technological know-how go hand-in-hand at ComputerCORP. The company continues to develop its structures and focus to service customers who now know what they want IT products to deliver.

Technology is at the heart of businesses, running processes and business critical applications as well as allowing information to be shared between customers, suppliers and employees. IT infrastructures need to be robust enough to cope with the demands of 24/7 availability, yet flexible enough to accommodate the latest developments for competitive advantage.

ComputerCORP staff help customers make the right choices and the company is committed to long-term partnerships that deliver real value to customers, whatever their changing needs.

Rather than outsourcing IT procurement and management services to reduce costs like many IT organisations, ComputerCORP has developed the delivery of business management services from conception to manage customer expectations and deliver high value desktop and infrastructure solutions, together with business critical solutions around storage, mobility, communications and security that are cost-effective and add value back into the business.

ComputerCORP aims to grow customer relationships into partnerships, taking a "big picture" approach to work collaboratively with customers for all their IT needs. The company provides hardware and fundamental commodity services including configuration and installation to desk, but its strategy is to focus on integrating services, developing tailored solutions and mixing and matching desktop business management services to respond effectively to the specific needs of each customer.

Offering customers a flexible choice is one of ComputerCORP's core values. The company is manufacturer independent so it provides cost-effective options with expert advice. The company has built up partnerships with some of the world's leading manufacturers and suppliers, such as IBM, HP, SUN Microsystems Toshiba, APC, Microsoft, Symantec, Cisco, Citrix, Redhat and Vodafone and they help ComputerCORP provide customers with their valued experience.

Right: With high level experience and expertise on the table, ComputerCORP brings a real world approach that sees customers obtain the most benefit from their IT expenditure.

ComputerCORP believes its main assets are its customers and the skills of its staff. The company works hard to attract and maintain talented staff and educates and motivates them to instil a positive service-oriented attitude and high standards. Engineers and sales staff work together to develop new services and solutions and the developing industry has required sales staff to expand their role to encompass an advisory service. ComputerCORP's service department represents half of the total staff employed at the company and the skilled technicians can deal with all customers' requirements.

The company operates to high standards and selects suppliers, people and processes with the aim of being the best. Building and maintaining organisational excellence is a long-term proposition that demands stability and vision. The company is committed to a culture of continuous improvement.

ComputerCORP has enjoyed financial stability with substantial and profitable growth. Considerable investment has been made into internal operations and the capacity of its logistics allows for location expansion and extensive growth in customer demand. The company developed software to streamline its systems to provide maximum customer satisfaction.

Having grown from a supplier of IT technology to a truly service and solution-orientated business, being acknowledged and rewarded by its vendor partners as being able to support and maintain their technology, ComputerCORP aims to continue to grow while delivering the best technology solutions to all its customers.

Above: Firmly focussed on maintaining service excellence, ComputerCORP's Technical Personnel are among the most accredited and professional IT Engineers in Australia.

HUMFREY LAND DEVELOPMENTS

Barry and Mary Humfrey founded their business in Geraldton to focus on property development in the mid-west. However, since its inception in 1988, Humfrey Land Developments has successfully completed projects from Exmouth to Dongara.

While many developers concentrate on the Perth metropolis, one couple has been busy creating thriving residential and tourist centres in regional WA.

Barry and Mary Humfrey's first success through Humfrey Land Developments was the transformation of barren, coastal scrub five kilometres from Geraldton into the award-winning residential development Seacrest Estate.

It has a reputation for high-quality affordable land and released lots have been selling fast.

Seacrest Estate is a total community, with provision for schools, recreation and commercial facilities, and is in Wandina, a suburb south of Geraldton in the Shire of Greenough. More than 600 lots have been developed and sold since the project started in 1999 and eventually about 1,260 lots will be developed.

Mr Humfrey said people wanted to live at Seacrest because it provided facilities unique in regional WA.

"All lots have fibre optic cabling to provide high-speed Internet services, movies on demand and enhanced TV reception," he said. "And a free computer is provided to each new dwelling, making this a technology estate."

The cabling also gives residents an opportunity to have home security and online education facilities, as well as the capacity to work from home.

The project is a joint venture between Springdale Holdings Pty Ltd (managed and operated by Humfrey Land Developments) and Landstart (Department of Housing and Works).

Mr Humfrey said there was a demand for housing in Geraldton because recent government and private infrastructure projects had created sustainable employment opportunities.

"We are also playing our part in providing other required infrastructure to cater for the increasing void in short-stay accommodation and conference facilities for the corporate market in the mid-west," he said.

"The availability of short-stay accommodation and resort-style complexes will also enable the mid-west tourism market to expand."

Mr Humfrey is involved with local tourism through his voluntary work as a board member of the Geraldton Visitor Centre and Australia's Coral Coast.

The Humfreys started HLD to project manage land sub-divisions, from the design stage through construction to individual lot sales.

The business's services cover property development, joint venture partnership for private and corporate clients and state and local government authorities, planning, subdivision design and feasibility studies.

In 2004, the Humfreys extended the business's project management activities to include holiday resort complexes. Mr Humfrey and a team of professional consultants are involved in the design and approval of developments including Mariner Resort in Geraldton and Norcape Lodge Resort in Exmouth.

The WA government recently appointed HLD as the preferred proponent to establish a sustainable nature-based tourist development at the Houtman Abrolhos Islands. All approvals for this project will be finalised by June 2006.

HLD started with three staff – Mr Humfrey, who has 35 years' land development experience, driving business operations, Mrs Humfrey controlling sales and a finance officer. This structure continued until February 2005, when a permanent project manager joined the team at its Foreshore Drive headquarters in The Marina, Geraldton.

Mr Humfrey said they created the new position to help with the hands-on management of budgets, contracts and project construction activities while working with engineers, contractors, surveyors and government authorities.

HLD's current projects include stages of Seacrest Residential Estate, Forrester Park Residential Estate, Batavia Gardens Estate, Mariner Resort Geraldton, North Cape Resort Exmouth, Exmouth Light Industrial Estate and Abrolhos Islands Resort of the Coast from Geraldton

Mr Humfrey said concept plans for Norcape Lodge Resort (situated on the town beach in Exmouth) were being developed for release in 2006 and the resort – consisting of 122 short-stay units, plus communal facilities such as a restaurant and conference centre – would be another significant project for the Gascoyne Region.

Other proposed ventures HLD will develop include a caravan and short-stay accommodation complex in Geraldton and the redevelopment of Geraldton Fishermen's Harbour, which will incorporate a significant Marine precinct and boat-lifting facilities.

Right: Managing director Barry Humfrey. Opposite page: (top) Seacrest Estate– one of Humfrey's major joint ventures; (bottom) our dedicated and qualified staff (left to right) Barry Humfrey, Glenn Hutton, Kel Turner and Mary Humfrey.

HLD has won many awards for its achievements. "We won an Urban Development Industry Association Award for Excellence in 1996 for a green street development known locally as Portacello Circle," Mr Humfrey said. "It was the first time this award was given to a project outside the metropolitan area."

Recent accolades include a Mid West Chamber of Commerce Small Business Award (fewer than five employees) 2005 and the West Australian Regional Small Business Awards Best Regional Micro Business 2005.

HLD also supports the community and industry it operates in, being a major sponsor of Geraldton Surf Lifesaving Club, the Master Builders Association Building Excellence Awards, the Geraldton Tennis Club 2006 Easter Open and a 2006 Rotary International District Conference in Geraldton.

Mr Humfrey said HLD planned to keep its office in Geraldton rather than moving to Perth.

"We want to give innovative developments to the people who have supported us over the years," he said.

"There are not enough large regional developers who keep their offices and employment opportunities in the country."

HLD has a reputation for being innovative and able to cater for community and government needs in creating opportunities for expanding markets, whether residential, industrial, commercial or for tourism operators.

The business's reputation now generates direct approaches for joint venture dealings.

Mr Humfrey said the HLD team ensured every project was analysed for suitability and sustainability and whether it would be needed by the general public, as well as commercial bodies.

"My company is able to read and define market directions in regional and remote areas," he said.

"Having a sound knowledge of the working systems and procedures of government authorities is also essential to success.

Most projects take years of planning – it took 17 years to gain approval for the Cape Wilderness Estate in Exmouth."

Mr Humfrey said the business hoped to build on its reputation as the pre-eminent developer of sustainable development within the mid-west that reflected the needs and aspirations of government and the community.

"We will continue to meet the demands for housing, industrial, commercial and tourism infrastructures in an efficient and viable means for the benefit of all stakeholders," he said.

AOT CONSULTING

Below: AOT Consulting is truly passionate about working with its clients and achieving excellent outcomes.

Many businesses have impressive stories about how they have grown with the developing state of Western Australia.

For more than 17 years, the consulting firm has provided its services to local, national and international clients and has played a key role in assisting corporate business and government to plan, implement and manage new initiatives.

The high quality of its professional services has ensured AOT Consulting itself has become a WA success story.

The firm provides independent business, management and technology professionals who achieve top results for its clients in the government and commercial sectors. Its specialist professional service consultants have a unique blend of sound commercial, business and technical expertise.

The firm is based in the Forrest Centre, 221 St Georges Terrace, Perth, and is owned and managed by founders David Taylor and Julie Faulkner.

The firm is truly passionate about working with its clients and achieving excellent outcomes for them.

Initially the firm diversified and explored different combinations of professional services which shaped the core business it provides today.

Its clients also helped to focus its strengths because of the types of services they were seeking from the firm.

Mr Taylor commented on the firm's initial business model. "We did not want to imitate other firms and researched contemporary management trends and models in strategic business planning and strategic procurement, which we have refined and refreshed over the years," he said.

As a result of having an excellent understanding of its client's needs and designing its professional services specifically to provide results that can be acted upon, AOT Consulting has created a service that represents true value.

A testament to this is that most of its business comes from repeat or referrals. AOT Consulting has always been focused on understanding client needs when planning and implementing new initiatives, reducing costs, managing risk, or examining the efficiency and effectiveness of existing business models, systems and processes.

The firm's independent advice is a key factor in this approach, allowing the outcomes to be defined based on the business requirement, giving an unbiased service.

As a leading provider of highly professional, independent quality consulting services that delivers results that can be acted upon, AOT Consulting is proud that it continues to maintain its uncompromising principles as it grows.

A key milestone for AOT Consulting in 1995 was to reinforce its commitment to delivering a quality service through working in accordance with its ISO 9001 Quality System, accredited by Bureau Veritas Quality International.

AOT Consulting's professional services are based upon quality processes. In the late 90s, it assisted in the planning of several strategic initiatives such as the popular OnlineWA and has since developed strategic plans, feasibility studies and business plans for many public and private organisations.

An area of the business that it continues to expand is strategic procurement planning and management, which it formalised in 1995 and which has since become a core service that the firm offers to its clients.

AOT Consulting has undertaken a significant number of strategic procurement planning and management projects since that time and has worked in various sectors including government, oil and gas, utilities, mining, information and communication technologies, science and technology, financial services, health, life sciences, education, law and order, sport and recreation, tourism and leisure.

Such diversification has led AOT Consulting to provide strategic probity and procurement advice on some of the state's high-value, high-risk initiatives.

Mr Taylor and Ms Faulkner share the executive management of the firm. To maintain its independence, the firm employs professionals rather than contracted staff.

Over the years, AOT Consulting has enjoyed compound growth in knowledge and experience which it always passes onto clients. Often, its starting point is well advanced and it can quickly focus in on helping clients achieve their business objectives.

Apart from operating a sustainable professional services firm since 1989, Mr Taylor and Ms Faulkner take pride in maintaining an ethical business that maintains professional standards while being pragmatic.

"Looking back at our history, we are most proud of contributing to the success of others by helping plan and implement initiatives while managing risks," Mr Taylor said.

AOT Consulting's mission is to be the best in helping others achieve their goals.

HYDRAMET AUSTRALIA

Hydramet Australia, a West Australian company, is respected nationally for its technical skill and innovative approach in designing and providing products, systems and services for water treatment and chemical metering applications.

Hydramet's products and services touch the lives of many people throughout Australia.

Though most may not recognise the brand name, Hydramet is well known to industry, business, utilities and government agencies and is respected for its dedication in creating systems that make water suitable for drinking, leisure use and other purposes.

This Australian success story began in WA in July 1989 when the company was founded to provide a range of equipment, technical services and specialist advice in water treatment and chemical metering technologies. It started with just three people operating from Belmont and delivering services to customers throughout the state. The three company founders, Jim Shaw, Peter Greene and Brenda Parasuraman, continue to be active members of the management team.

Since 1989, the company has grown and now serves a geographically broad base of customers throughout WA from Argyle in the north to Esperance in the south. It has also expanded into South Australia where the Adelaide branch was established in 1996 and, more recently, to Victoria where the Melbourne branch was opened in 2002.

The company's main lines of business include systems for making water safe and healthy for drinking; systems for keeping swimming pools safe, clean and enjoyable; systems for disinfecting water used in food processing plants; and systems for processing waste water to make it safe for returning to the environment.

The family-owned business employs almost 40 people and has the resources to design, construct, test, install and commission entire systems to customers' unique requirements. Hydramet also provides assistance to the emergency services and works with them whenever they respond to emergencies in areas where the chemical chlorine is stored and used.

Throughout the years, Hydramet has kept its headquarters in WA. Today, it operates from large premises in Canning Vale and has become an industry leader in the provision of services and technologies within the water industry.

Most companies encounter obstacles along their paths to success and Hydramet was no exception, according to managing director Jim Shaw.

"Among the obstacles to innovation that the company had to overcome was the difficulty of finding people with the specialist knowledge, skills and experience required to create solutions and provide a full level of service to our customers," Mr Shaw said.

"There were not too many people around with these skills when the company started. We are committed to training our team members and we chose to deal with the shortage of qualified people by developing our employees' skills and knowledge using in-house training programs.

"We decided to provide trade apprenticeships and now offer young people the opportunity to train as water treatment technical specialists while learning the electrical trade and obtaining an electrical trade qualification. This approach has proven successful for Hydramet and our apprentices have gained the opportunity to develop valuable industry experience."

The first tradesman to graduate from the apprenticeship program, in 2003, now represents Hydramet as a professional technician.

The company has also developed training programs specific to the industry and makes these available to customers. Among the technologies

Right: Hydramet founder and managing director Jim Shaw (right) with sales manager Clint Hall in the company's new Research & Development and Demonstration Centre. This facility is used for product and technology development as well as training and demonstration purposes.

in which Hydramet staff are trained and actively participate are chlorination, fluoridation, water softening, UV treatment, reverse osmosis, filtration and chemical metering systems. Hydramet recently installed and commissioned a dissolved air flotation process for Alcoa to facilitate waste water recovery.

To ensure the continuation of the company's capabilities to provide innovative solutions into the future, the company opened the Hydramet Research & Development and Demonstration Centre in 2005.

"This investment provides the facilities and environment for Hydramet staff to turn ideas into products and systems and to develop and refine them for applications," said technical services manager Peter Greene.

One of the key factors contributing to Hydramet's success is its focus on serving the interests of all its stakeholders. The company considers the impact of its activities on customers, employees, suppliers, the public as well as the shareholders and makes its corporate decisions from a stakeholder point of view.

Customers turn to Hydramet to develop solutions for their needs with the knowledge that Hydramet can develop and deliver enduring, high quality results and will continue to invest in its capabilities. Engineered-to-order systems are a significant part of the range of services available and customers know that Hydramet has the skills and resources to maintain these in perfect working order and to provide very rapid response to any breakdowns.

Employees are provided with first-class employment terms and conditions. They are rewarded for pursuing excellence in customer service by participating in the company's profits.

Suppliers represented by Hydramet are chosen for the quality of their products and Hydramet provides them with access to the market and the benefits of long-term relationships. Many such continuing relationships date back to the founding days of the company.

The public benefits from the quality of the equipment and systems Hydramet selects for their protection and enjoyment as well as from the company's responsible approach to the environmental impact of its operations. The company's care for the environment was evident recently in King's Park where Hydramet installed a new water treatment plant for the Water Corporation at the Mount Eliza reservoir, demonstrating all due consideration to the sensitivity of the area. This plant was built in the company's facility at Canning Vale and delivered to site as an operable system.

Hydramet is proud to have its headquarters in WA, a somewhat unusual home for a company providing product and support services across all of Australia. The company is widely recognised throughout the industry for its skill and innovative approach and provides economic benefit to the state through its exports.

Mr Shaw attributes success to several factors: "Hydramet has a high business ethic, a strong sense of responsibility, good financial stability, a vast level of skill and experience in the team, and can demonstrate a solid base of company experience covering more than 17 years in WA."

Above: A bird's eye view of the service shop and the indoor construction area. The two portable buildings being fitted out will be delivered to site as complete water treatment plants. Hydramet's facility also includes an outdoor construction area with capacity for an additional 12 treatment plants.

Left: Senior technician Dave Gligurovski conducts tests on a control panel as part of system validation. These control units are designed in-house using a CAD system. The control logic is achieved using electrical control systems and software-controlled electronics.

Name any brand or type of earthmoving equipment and it is a fair bet it will be sitting at Action Mining Services, being refurbished to be sent back to work at a remote mine site.

But like many of the leaders in the West Australian resources industry, Mr de Mol has no time for play in the middle of a mining boom, he is flat-out making sure his company can keep up with the increasing demand from contractors and miners throughout the state.

"The machines we receive to repair and refurbish are desperately needed by their owners to keep production going, so there is intense pressure on us to return them to site promptly," Mr de Mol said.

Any visitor who goes to Action Mining Services multi-million dollar workshop and massive machinery yard at Hazelmere, near the Perth airport, should take a close look at the photo of Mr de Mol's original operation. The photo of him leaning against his mobile sandblasting truck demonstrates better than a thousand words just how far the company has come since its formation as Action Blast in 1992.

The Action Mining Services' yard contains more than 100 pieces of equipment including some of the biggest excavators and dump trucks used anywhere in the world. They have been transported in one piece or, because of their size, broken into many components and sent to Mr de Mol's facility for repair and refurbishment.

Up to 400 hours of intensive work later they leave the yard blasted, repaired, improved and glistening with new paint. It's hard to believe an operation of this scale has been created in just 14 years by a single owner

with no formal business training or experience. Yet the figures speak for themselves and Action Mining Services now has a 70 percent share of the market for servicing, repairing, refurbishing and quarantine cleaning of earthmoving equipment in Western Australia. Such a share of the earthmoving market may not be significant in other parts of the world but in WA, where mining is a multi-billion dollar industry, it is big business.

"It explains why there is so much pressure on us from customers, At this point in time they are trying to extend as much life and value as possible out of their existing earthmoving equipment, because new equipment is in very short supply and getting increasingly more expensive" Mr de Mol said.

While it is often the big names in mining that take the glory during a resources boom, there is no doubt those producers could not operate with the unsung heroes like Mr de Mol and his team who help support their mines operating day after day.

"Our team are now helping much of Western Australia's mining industry keep up with the demand from China and elsewhere for our minerals by keeping their fleets of trucks and excavators working," Mr de Mol said.

"I would never pretend that we have been an overnight success. There has been a lot of hard work to get to this point and it is has not always been good times in our industry. Much of my time in the mining industry has been in a downturn.

"For the team that runs the company, one of our proudest achievements was to continue offering apprenticeships during those leaner times when most of the mining industry gave up on providing trade training.

"It doesn't matter whether economic conditions have been rain, hail or shine we've always kept our apprenticeships going. With another 15 teenagers part way through or completing their training this year. "

As with all entrepreneurial activities, the business has not all been plain sailing since the company was established.

"In the early 1990s I had three mobile sandblasting units which were in high demand to help repair earthmoving equipment," Mr de Mol said. As more information became available about the health and safety issues with sandblasting the demand for mobile services dried up, better facilities were needed to meet new regulations and standards.

Others might have changed their business altogether but Mr de Mol adapted to the new regime and moved forward. His next step was to buy an industrial property in Hazelmere and construct a quarantine wash, blast, paint and repair facility. The most important requirement for the new facility was that it could safely clean and repair equipment without any adverse environmental effects.

"Business took off again and by 1998 our team had doubled to 50 as demand escalated for services that only we seemed to be providing to organisations with earthmoving equipment," Mr de Mol said.

That original Hazelmere site contained a one-stop shop catering to every element of repair work for earthmoving equipment and quarantine cleaning of imported machinery. This was vital to keep up with demand from miners, ranging from iron ore to gold producers.

"We put on double shifts 4 years ago to keep pace with the needs of our clients, however the move to greater outsourcing meant demand kept increasing," Mr de Mol said.

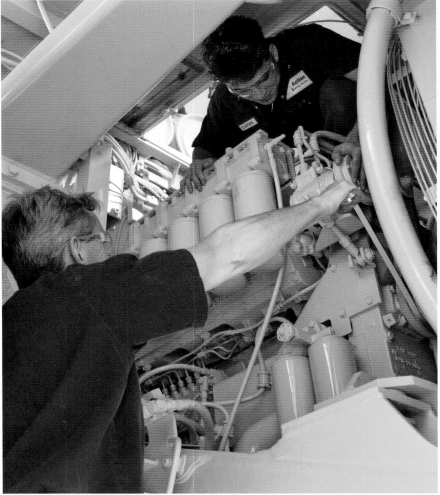

"Eventually in 2004 we reached a point where we had to build a much bigger facility to match both the increasing demand and the increasing size of the equipment being repaired.

"A decade ago we were refurbishing 100-tonne dump trucks, now we are rebuilding 300-tonne dump trucks. It didn't take a mathematician to realise that our workshop had to get much bigger to accommodate the new range of equipment."

Mr de Mol built a workshop with 6,000sqm of undercover space and doors eight metres wide and 14m high on an adjoining property. There are not many mobile machines apart from aircraft that can not fit into the building. The workshop also has two 10-tonne overhead cranes and other heavy duty equipment to strip machines for repair or quarantine washing. While moving premises, Mr de Mol changed the company name from Action Blast to Action Mining Services, to better reflect the much wider range of services the company was offering to clients.

"We were providing every conceivable equipment repair service to clients, yet our old name made it sound like we specialized in one thing, so it was time to change our identity to better reflect our services," Mr de Mol said. Action Mining Services now provides a comprehensive mechanical and component repair service for all types of earthmoving equipment, from the repair of minor oil leaks through to the complete rebuild of machinery and components.

"Our team can repair, rebuild or refurbish equipment from leading brands like Caterpillar, Liebherr, Komatsu, Hitachi and Terex," Mr de Mol said. Action Mining Services is also able to source the best prices for parts because it does not have dealer restrictions. It can also gain access to quality generic and after-market parts that lead to significant cost-savings for clients.

The company offers a comprehensive metal fabrication service for earthmoving equipment that includes boiler making, welding, cab refurbishments, tray rebuilds, bucket repairs and general panel fabrication. Action also offers an in-house inline boring service – a cost effective alternative to either dismantling equipment to be repaired or outsourcing to other suppliers.

One of the reasons for building the new workshop was to increase the amount of equipment that could be refurbished at one time. Four machines can now be sandblasted simultaneously in the weatherproof blast booth. Depending on their size, several pieces of earthmoving equipment can now be painted simultaneously in the 640sqm spray booths.

Even though it has its huge workshop and yard, the Action Mining Service team are also highly mobile and operate all over the state. "We bring most of the equipment we are repairing to Perth because our specialist tools, equipment and parts are here," Mr de Mol said. "However, sometimes we will travel to remote sites to undertake specific projects to refurbish client's equipment."

The company has a field service fleet to get machinery working as soon as possible and avoid the costs that come with down-time.

In what is now a global industry, Action's work is not just limited to WA. Mr de Mol and his team regularly manage the preparation and packaging of any mining equipment and machinery, from excavators to dump trucks, for road or shipping transportation to anywhere i n Australia or overseas.

Because Action Mining Services is now a global industry player, part of its challenge is to stay at the forefront of development during a time of high demand and shortages of equipment and skills.

"I recently went to China to find manufacturers of after-market parts such as cab seats so we could provide extra value for our customers," Mr de Mol said.

"I take the view that it is not up to our customers to tell me how we could better help them. It's up to our team to present them with ideas and opportunities that will extend their equipment life or at least deliver savings."

So how do you build WA's largest earthmoving repair company from scratch in just over a decade? Through hard work and a love of challenges at least that seems to be Mr de Mol's successful recipe.

Below: Three of the 17 trucks completed for HWE Indonesia.

He comes from a family with no business background and said they were surprised when he kept expanding his small Action Blast business. "They weren't alone in thinking I was taking big risks because there was no sign of a mining boom at that time."

"Of course, like all business people, I was taking risks but it is easier to see the logic behind it now that the rewards are also visible. Fortunately, I had traveled a lot and that had opened my eyes to possibilities and once I had decided to follow a growth path there was no going back. "There is a lot to be said for staying small and profitable, rather than being large and broke. It's the old saying – turnover is vanity, while the bottom line is sanity.

"I think Action Mining Services has arrived at a very good point somewhere between the two. We are large enough to be the key player in our market but still a niche company in the overall mining industry. This means we still feel like a smaller business with a very close-knit and professional team."

The transition from employee to business owner has taught Mr de Mol valuable lessons. "There are three key elements to being successful. You must have a balanced life, create a culture in your organisation that will be strong enough to enable the business to run smoothly in your absence, and you must be profitable enough to continue to grow and reinvest in

the business to continue providing the service and opportunities your customers and employees require," Mr de Mol said.

These are insights gained over many years in building a successful business. Mr de Mol, a former finalist in Ernst & Young's Entrepreneur of the Year Awards, still believes there is a lot left to learn.

"This is a very demanding business and you have to give it everything you've got, particularly in the current boom conditions. My hope is that over time I'll also be able to explore new opportunities in mining and other industries," he said.

Of course, if he ever has more time for play, there are always plenty of toys in his backyard.

Above: Fabricating bulldozer blades.

CREATING COMMUNITIES

It's an irony of modern life that the more emphasis there is on the global community the less connected we are with our own.

But the vagaries associated with globalization are in turn causing a renewed interest in what's closest to home.

Award-winning consultancy Creating Communities Australia is a firm committed to inspiring its clients to get involved in the 'art of building the local community', so that people thrive at the local level.

Formed in 1992, Creating Communities is dedicated to blending the needs and aspirations of business, community members and stakeholders to create vibrant and functional local communities.

"Community is about people. It's about people living and working in an environment they can relate to," explains company director Donna Shepherd.

"It's about careful consideration of all the aspects of our existence, including creating a local economy. This in turn helps drive that community's cultural and social life," she adds.

Below: Celebrate.

This holistic approach to planning reemerged at Rio Earth Summit in the early 1990s, which suggested sustainability required a balance of positive social, ecological and economical outcomes.

"When our lives revolved around the same place, community evolved more naturally. This is now less likely to happen and the Rio Summit was a timely realty check for us all. The challenge now is how to respond," says Ms Shepherd.

With a diverse array of clients, including the state's top land developers, the mining sector, government agencies and not-for-profit organisations, the company has developed a unique approach that is about creating communities from opportunities.

"We focus on aspirations and outcomes in order to create a shared vision that is values driven," says fellow director Allan Tranter.

"Having an exciting picture of the future means that issues become speed humps along the way rather than an end in themselves. The models that we have developed can be applied to a wide range of environments.

"By unearthing a uniquely distinctive character for a community as part of the initiating process, Creating Communities has been able to focus people's energy on working together to achieve positive outcomes throughout each project," he says.

Part of this process involves analysis of demographics, quality of life, wellness, the local economy and services and facilities. It is during this phase that key relationships are established.

A series of stakeholder workshops are often held to draw out areas of mutual benefit between stakeholders. This is then used to develop an overarching vision for the project's goals and initiatives.

The multidisciplinary team, skilled in areas as diverse as sociology, sport and recreation, public relations, urban planning, psychology, population health, diversity and estates/facility management, then moves into the activation phase.

"The relevance of the methodology comes from an understanding that communities do not evolve from physical determinants alone," says Ms Sheperd.

"They need productive working relationships between stakeholders and local community-led organisations to activate, celebrate and utilise the physical form that contemporary urban planning has sought to deliver," she adds.

The company's approach also centres on identifying local characteristics that can be used to build partnerships between various stakeholders to deliver a benefit that is both creative and innovative.

"Through this, residents and businesses are provided with the physical and social foundations to build a self-sustaining community," explains Mr Tranter.

"And the basis for this is the formation of stakeholder relationships and partnerships."

Fostering open dialogue between groups ensures a range of opportunities are created, from which partnerships, coordinated service delivery and a shared-service provision can then emerge.

The natural environment is also central to the company's initiatives.

"We consistently seek to enhance the quality of the natural environment by identifying opportunities for community involvement in local projects," he says.

"And we often look to develop and facilitate a range of environmental awareness programs and initiatives to encourage a shared sense of responsibility for the neighbourhood."

Though the scope of their methodology is diverse the overarching ethos Creating Communities applies to all its projects is ensuring that strategies are appropriate and outcome-based, so initiatives are both meaningful and practical.

"Communities are diverse so our approach must be too," he says.

Research recently carried out by Victoria's Deakin University indicates that where Creating Communities has played a central role, individuals have a statistically significantly higher than average Personal Wellbeing Index (health, relationships, feelings of safety and security, life satisfaction) compared to surrounding neighbourhoods and the Australian national average.

A similar pattern has also emerged for Neighbourhood Indices (trust, social participation, sharing and borrowing, attitudes to environment, common goals and values) and National Wellbeing Indices (state of the environment, business, government and security).

Above: Recreate. Top: Interact.

"It's not just facilities or services that creates a community, it's things like establishing community groups, bringing people together through events and activities, and giving them the tools so they can not only solve their own problems but become empowered in a way that can affect their future lives," says Mr Tranter.

"What this research shows is that it's a holistic and deliberate approach to community development that works. This in turn results in an increased level of satisfaction within the communities we're engaged in, and provides a competitive edge for our clients whose business is people."

WA BUSINESS NEWS

WA Business News is as unique as the West Australian business landscape it examines every week, spawned in an isolated environment that was starved of local market intelligence with an independent viewpoint.

There is nothing quite like this newspaper anywhere in Australia; a publication that puts serious, state-based news in a compelling weekly format.

The newspaper – and its complimentary daily email news service – offers WA business people and interested outsiders a unique perspective on issues that matter to them in their state.

"Our core focus is to be parochially West Australian and provide information that people need to know in the operation of their businesses," publisher Harry Kleyn said.

He said the newspaper not only helped the WA business community stay informed with news it would not easily find elsewhere, but had an ambassadorial role to highlight matters that concerned commerce and industry.

Part of that mission requires the newspaper to reach smaller business operators in the suburbs and industrial areas as well as corporate city high-flyers.

Mr Kleyn, a founder of Community Newspaper Group, established *WA Business News* in 1993.

"I had been out of the newspaper business for five years but this was a good reason to return – there was no business-focused paper in WA," Mr Kleyn said.

WA Business News began as a free fortnightly newspaper circulated almost exclusively in the Perth CBD and has evolved into a state-wide, paid subscription-model publication.

In 2000, Elton Swarts became executive director when he bought into the business and the pair soon embarked on a study tour in America to help further propel the publication.

"That was a watershed; in America our type of publication was a mature model of media and every town had a paid weekly business publication," Mr Kleyn explained.

"Content was all-important because business readers are time-poor and impatient – they want compelling, significant information."

The pair developed a strategic plan, and soon went weekly backed by the appointment of prominent WA business writer Mark Pownall as editor. He was resourced to build up the editorial team to create a formidable business newsroom.

An evolution of the plan saw a direct subscriber model put in place, backed by a team of dedicated telemarketers.

"That has been very successful and we have had consistent growth since launching that model three years ago," Mr Kleyn said.

"We have more than 64,600 readers and 91 percent of those are decision-makers in their organisation."

Below: (front left to right) events and sponsorship manager Michelle Natta, subscriptions manager Allison Carins, and publisher Harry Kleyn; (back left to right) editor Mark Pownall, sales manager Peter Montague, financial controller Ian Swarts and executive director Elton Swarts.

A Nielsen Media Research 2005 readers' survey found 70 percent of readers believed *WA Business News* was a "must read" for their business.

"They see it as a great source of business information and it is highly appreciated in the marketplace," Mr Kleyn said.

"I am very proud that people who used to receive the paper free were willing to pay to subscribe. It is a huge endorsement of how they value the product."

"Marketing professionals tell us that one paid paper is equivalent to five free ones in terms of marketing."

In July 2003, the paper beat a large international field to win a bronze prize at the Alliance of Area Business Publication's Annual Editorial Excellence Awards.

Mr Kleyn said the Alliance represented 65 business-focused publications world-wide and the award recognised *WA Business News'* high standards against competition that had been around for much longer.

Judges stated that *WA Business News* was a publication "with attitude, bold in content and design and, therefore, well-suited for the region it serves".

That win proved no fluke when *WA Business News* won two awards at the 2005 AABP Editorial Excellence Awards conference – the bronze award for best small tabloid and bronze for best scoop.

The newspaper, of course, is no stranger to awards. Since 2002 it has developed its own awards programs to honour local business achievers.

As a result, events have become a complementary focus for *WA Business News*. It began with the launch of what is now the publisher's signature event, the *WA Business News* 40under40 awards program, which recognises successful business operators throughout the state.

In five years it has honoured 200 outstanding West Australians from all fields of business and beyond. In 2005 the awards night attracted almost 900 guests.

"It has become one of the business community's most anticipated annual gala awards night and we recognise talent and individuals that might not otherwise be honoured because the awards are not industry-specific," Mr Kleyn explained.

But events are not the only field where this organisation has kept a step ahead of the traditional media. In news gathering it has sought to use the latest technology to spread the local word.

In November 2005, *WA Business News* introduced breaking news announcements on its website, complemented with a free daily email service in the late afternoon.

With a news environment that was shifting with technological change, Mr Kleyn said it was a way for the weekly publication to keep readers up-to-date with timely news, and it had already attracted 7,730 subscribers.

"It allows us to reach a lot of people who may not necessarily be exposed to the traditional newspaper," he said.

WA Business News editor Mark Pownall said the emails added another level of credibility to the news team.

Above: WA Business News running off the press in East Victoria Park.

"In a weekly paper we will not publish information that is 'old news' – that meant we used to have to ignore a lot of what was going on and concentrate on giving our readers something different," he explained.

"But the daily email allows us to cover everything and prove we know what's happening in the business world."

Mr Kleyn said *WA Business News* had built a strong loyal readership and was attracting solid advertising support from large corporates covering sections such as airlines, banks, recruiters, business services and the IT industries.

"*WA Business News* is a unique and valuable vehicle for business to gain weekly access to the decision-makers in the WA market," Mr Kleyn said.

Based in its heartland, in the Perth CBD on Beaufort Street, *WA Business News* now has 35 employees.

Mr Kleyn said the paper would remain as a weekly but he planned to expand the online side of the business.

"We live in an exciting state and I believe *WA Business News* can play a prominent part in business decisions and information dissemination," he said.

TOWN OF VICTORIA PARK

The traditional Labor working-class area, which had former WA Premier Geoff Gallop as its state member, has been attracting a young, trendy demographic with its recent up-market residential and commercial developments.

Despite its relative youth as a municipality – originally formed in 1897 it was dissolved into the City of Perth from 1917 to 1993 before being proclaimed in 1994 – the town offers a range of high-quality services and facilities for more than 28,000 residents.

Town residents can stay in the area for leisure, shopping and nightlife, enjoying the local facilities. There is the Gurney VC RSL & Community Centre, Victoria Park Library, the recently redeveloped Aqualife Centre (formerly known as Somerset Street Swimming Pool) and the Leisurelife Centre, as well as parks, shops, cafes, restaurants and bars.

For those who want to venture further, the Town of Victoria Park is only minutes south from Perth city.

Chief executive John Bonker said councillors and staff had worked hard to create an inclusive community for residents and business operators.

"We want people to take pride in the town and identify it as a great and unique place to be," he said.

Creative endeavours are encouraged, in 1995 the town created the annual Victoria Park Art Awards and the Spring Gardens Competition.

Residents and their friends can enjoy free summer twilight concerts at local parks and reserves and youth are catered for at the free all-ages YAC-A-TOA festival.

Organised by the town's Youth Advisory Council, Perth musicians perform annually for YAC-A-TOA on the banks of the Swan River at McCallum Park.

Mr Bonker said the town welcomed its new citizens at an annual Australia Day Citizenship Ceremony and those who helped make the community a better place were honoured at an annual Volunteers Morning Tea.

Mr Bonker said the town received a High Commendation from the Customer Service Council of WA in 2005.

"The entire organisation has a commitment to always doing the right thing, ethically, morally, legally and professionally," he said.

"We know our community and value their views and involvement in the work we do on a daily basis.

"By keeping one step ahead of emerging trends, needs and opportunities and providing very professional service, the town's staff have established themselves as leaders in the provision of quality customer service."

Community consultation is important to the town, Mr Bonker said.

"We have a discussion forum on our website and teenagers are encouraged to join or pass on their views to the Youth Advisory Council," he said.

"We keep the community informed through regular newsletters and recently introduced a business newsletter to keep our valuable local businesses informed about issues affecting them."

The recently refurbished administration centre is on Shepperton Road, in Victoria Park, where 139 full or part-time employees are based.

Mr Bonker said the town developed a strategic plan in 2004 that would take it to 2013.

"Our vision includes promoting community development, enhancing the natural environment and supporting sustainable economic growth," he said.

The council had also worked hard to improve traffic safety and aesthetics of the area, putting in roundabouts, replacing footpaths, installing automatic irrigation systems on reserves and moving to underground power.

Mr Bonker said each December, more than 40 emergency service vehicles travelled through the town to raise awareness about road safety during the Christmas holiday period.

With a mix of residential, commercial and industrial properties, the town caters to a diverse mix of constituents.

The Town of Victoria Park comprises the suburbs of Victoria Park, East Victoria Park, St James, Carlisle, Lathlain, Burswood, and parts of Bentley and Welshpool.

Mr Bonker said he was proud of the way Mayor Mick Lee, councillors and staff ran the town.

"Our people – elected members and appointed staff – work together in a spirit of friendship and harmony to deliver quality services to an appreciative community," he said.

Top: Community concert with the West Australian Symphony Orchestra at Burswood Park.
Above: Mayor Mick Lee and the Fraga family at the Australia Day 2006 citizenship ceremony.

WESTNET

Westnet is among the five fastest-growing internet service providers (ISP) in the country and is on its way to achieving its aim of being the best in Australia.

Offering dial-up and broadband (DSL) internet, web hosting and telephony services to homes and businesses, Westnet focuses on providing high quality, competitively priced, internet products combined with exceptional customer service.

Chris Thomas, now head of Westnet's research and development team, established Westnet Internet Services in December 1994. The company's primary goals were to give local residents dial-up internet access for the cost of a local call, then expand that service throughout WA.

It became the first ISP to provide this internet coverage statewide and continues to invest in the promotion of internet services in rural areas. This has significantly contributed to user acceptance and the uptake of internet technology throughout regional Australia.

In 1996, Mitchell & Brown bought Westnet and in 1999, relocated it to Perth. Shortly afterwards, the arrival of broadband internet and the consequent market acceptance and uptake of high-speed internet proved to be a significant milestone for Westnet and the commercial internet landscape.

Westnet's operations expanded to encompass broadband internet, with telephony, web hosting and domain registration services also added to its product stable.

Although these products and services experienced significant growth and success, the company's most successful initiative was the provision of unrivalled customer service.

It is renowned for its high level of customer satisfaction, combined with reliability and accessibility of internet service. It has received national awards that recognise its efforts to be an industry leader in both these areas.

Accolades include achieving the highest level of customer satisfaction for ISPs in both the 16th and 17th ACNielsen Consult Australian Online Survey 2004, being named the ISP with the best network reliability in the Australian Broadband Survey 2004 and voted the best for customer service in the 2003 and 2004 Australian Broadband Surveys. Westnet also won the 2004 WA Information Technology and Telecommunications Awards service delivery and training award.

Managing director Peter Brown said customer service had always been a driving philosophy, so to receive various awards and become the recognised industry leader in that area had exceeded the company's founding expectations.

In recent years, Westnet has enjoyed impressive subscriber growth, which has fuelled organisational expansion. Mr Brown said one of the biggest challenges the company faced was recruiting and training staff at a rate equal to its growth.

"We want to increase our customer service staff numbers to maintain an industry-leading service staff-to-customer ratio and our reputation for friendly person-to-person customer service," he said.

Members of Westnet's Sales, Technical Support and Accounts departments undergo extensive, continual training to develop their customer service skills, ensuring the company's exceptionally high standards are not only maintained, but improved upon.

Right: Managing director Peter Brown is guiding Westnet through an exciting and dynamic period in the Australian telecommunications industry.

The company's recruiting efforts are aided by its reputation as a favoured employer in the industry, with a great culture among staff and a highly social, enjoyable work environment.

"We are very lucky to have such incredible staff morale and it is gratifying to be able to say that our staff members are our greatest asset. The benefit of great mateship among staff is invaluable and this has been part of Westnet's culture from day one," Mr Brown said.

The company has also been extremely successful in establishing strong relationships with local communities through its extensive agent network.

Westnet agents provide the ISP with presence in various communities across Australia and have further enabled Westnet to achieve the delivery of its products and exemplary service directly to the marketplace.

Mr Brown said one of the company's early goals was to develop Westnet from an internet provider into a complete telecommunications company. It launched Westnet Phone in 2004, initially offering only long-distance and international call plans, but in 2006, expanded to encompass full service phone products that include line rental and service on all phone calls.

"By launching Westnet Phone in a full service capacity, we hope to gain a competitive foothold in the telephony market that we hope translates to further organisational growth," Mr Brown said.

"I believe we are now able to compete more effectively with larger corporations in the marketplace."

He said the move was also motivated by trends that indicated customers wanted to use one provider for their phone and internet products, meaning one bill for both services.

"Simplicity is a major factor in customers' purchasing decisions in the telco sector," he said.

He expected strong growth in the company's phone business because of the interest its internet customers had shown in the full service products.

"We hope that many of our internet customers recognise that we can now deliver a complete phone and internet solution," he said.

Westnet's managing director said that in the continually evolving telecommunications landscape, customers would soon look for telcos that could provide internet, phone, media and entertainment products.

"Customers are looking harder than ever to find a complete solution for their communications needs and I believe service providers that can offer a diverse product range, and thus a complete service solution, stand the best chance of performing well in a rapidly changing business environment," he said.

Westnet will work to continue its rise as one of the country's premier ISPs and become a household name in the telephony market, where it aims to build a successful customer base with the same service values.

Above: The convergence of internet, telephone and media technologies will continue to present a number of opportunities for Westnet as it looks to connect customers to constantly evolving communications products.

Top: Westnet's focus on the delivery of friendly, person-to-person customer service has been instrumental in establishing itself as one of the country's premier ISPs.

WATER CORPORATION

From a commanding position on Fremantle's Victoria Quay, the life-size bronze statue of Charles Yelverton O'Connor maintains a constant vigil over the brilliant engineer's first major contribution to the development of Western Australia – Fremantle Harbour.

The statue of the man who arguably almost single-handedly pushed Western Australia into the 20th century faces away from the Darling Range east of Perth where O'Connor was to undertake a scheme of even more noble proportions that would revolutionise life in the Goldfields – but end his own.

'CY', as he is forever immortalised to generations of engineers worldwide who regard him as one of their greatest ever, went on from his Fremantle Harbour triumph to design and, for the most part, guide the construction of the Goldfields Water Supply Scheme – known to this day as the Goldfields Pipeline, transporting water from Mundaring Weir outside Perth 560km to Kalgoorlie-Boulder in the heart of WA's Goldfields.

The official opening of the Goldfields Pipeline on January 22, 1903 remains a defining moment in the history of water infrastructure development in this state and has inspired engineers and dozens of others in specialist callings to follow in the footsteps of their great construction leader to this day.

For O'Connor, it was a time of trial and tribulation. He came under severe criticism as his scheme was variously described in the media of the day, political circles and in other quarters as foolhardy, impractical, a waste of public money – and worse. The fierce criticism and the strain proved too much for O'Connor and he took his own life at South Fremantle on March 10, 1902.

However, the indomitable spirit, guts and breathtaking engineering skills that led to the long-cherished pioneering dream of getting water to the Goldfields was picked up by a succession of engineers over the next 100

years, all imbued with the burning desire to ensure WA's water services met the demands of industry and a rapidly growing population.

Fast forward exactly 100 years to 2002, with the south-west corner of Western Australia in the grip of an enduring and extremely severe drought. The parallels with O'Connor's situation a century before were eerily similar.

O'Connor's problem was that there was no water in the Goldfields where virtually all the state's wealth was coming from at that time. An enduring solution was required and he achieved that objective in spectacular style.

In 2002, the Water Corporation was faced with an equally great challenge – a debilitating drought and evidence of a drying climate. Like O'Connor, they came up with a suite of options as an enduring solution that later became known as the 'Security through Diversity' program to secure WA's water future. In an ironic twist, two years later in 2004 as an early component of this program, the WA government and the Water Corporation announced that the next major water source for Perth would be a seawater desalination plant – the first in Australia. Echoing the past, the news of a desalination plant was greeted in some quarters as being as controversial as the development of the Goldfields Pipeline.

And in a further irony, the government confirmed that the desalination plant would build the water factory on the Kwinana Industrial Strip close to where CY O'Connor ended his life.

While CY O'Connor was the catalyst who thrust water supply into a public debate that has endured through to this century, the history of this essential service to Western Australia actually began in 1890. At the start of 1996, the Water Corporation opened for business after more than a century-long metamorphosis from the original Waterworks Board, through various incarnations such as Metropolitan Water, Sewerage and Drainage Supply, Public Works (covering the entire state), Metropolitan Water Board and Water Authority.

Below: The Goldfields water pipeline – one of Western Australia's greatest engineering achievements.

Below right: Construction of the Perth Seawater Desalination plant, a new major water source, was greeted by some as controversial.

The corporatised utility today is one of the state government's foremost business agencies and is without doubt among the leading water utilities in Australia.

While it gathers great strength from, and has enormous pride in, the remarkable efforts of its illustrious predecessors, the Water Corporation has its collective eye focused firmly on the future of a booming state.

In short, it is charged firmly with the responsibility of ensuring the state's water supply future for coming generations against a backdrop of a drying climate. It has an equally compelling responsibility to ensure the growing wastewater stream into the future is either recycled or disposed of safely and without environmental harm.

Closer to Western Australia's two million people, perhaps, is the utility's responsibility for providing water and wastewater infrastructure that 24 hours a day and night ensures that drinking water reaches homes and businesses and wastewater is removed for treatment. These responsibilities, together with the necessity and an enthusiasm to provide water infrastructure for major developments clearly demonstrates that the Water Corporation – as was its predecessors – is one of the great infrastructure developers in WA.

Geographically, the Corporation is the largest water services utility in the world with responsibility for towns in vastly different temperature zones and astonishing diverse climatic conditions covering one third of the Australian continent. A prime example of the climatic diversity that tests the skills and resources of the Water Corporation and other WA agencies, sometimes close to the very limits of their abilities, is the annual cyclone season. It is not uncommon for a cyclone itself to wreak major damage to a town and its infrastructure from its 'eye' if it crosses the coast with an unfortunate northern WA town in its sights. Then it can turn into a torrential rain-bearing depression that can (and has) caused major flooding problems for Corporation engineers and myriad other specialists in towns and farmland areas deep into the south of the state.

The two million people relying on the Corporation's 24/7 services are spread across 2.5 million square kilometres of one of the driest countries on earth. Servicing an area four and a half times the size of Texas has ensured that the Water Corporation is one of Australia's largest water-service providers, with an asset base of about $10 billion.

The full extent of its services takes in the provision of water, wastewater and drainage services to homes, business and industry throughout WA. Additionally, it is a bulk supplier of water for irrigation, again in diverse areas from Kununurra in the far north to the Preston Valley in the south west. The Corporation directly employs more than 2,000 people and has generated revenues of more than $1 billion a year in recent times.

The majority of its profits are returned to the Western Australian government as a dividend to contribute to the development of the state. Unlike almost all other organisations, the Corporation still has fully operational centres in six regional centres – Karratha, Geraldton, Northam, Kalgoorlie Boulder, Albany, Bunbury – and in Perth itself, making it a truly statewide operation in the fullest sense of the word.

In Western Australia's south-west corner, where most of the state's people live, the Water Corporation ignited the interest of all other Australian states following a WA government decision in late July 2004 to build the southern hemisphere's first seawater desalination plant. The utility shaped up to the number one challenge facing governments and water planners in many parts of the world – how to secure longterm drinking water supplies in a clearly drying climate.

Western Australia was not the only Australian state in the first decade of the 2000s to suffer heavily from the effects of a prolonged and widespread drought and now ongoing climate change that continues to make life tough for water planners and many specialists in other fields.

What separated WA from its eastern seaboard counterparts, was the indisputable fact that the effects of the drought and the drying climate hit its south west corner in the years following the start of this century faster and harder than anywhere else in the country.

Above: The Woodman Point Wastewater Treatment Plant treats and safely disposes of wastewater from all suburbs south of Perth's Swan River. The ongoing need to provide major water infrastructure across Western Australia makes the Water Corporation one of the state's great infrastructure developers.

Right: Perth is the centre of the Integrated Water Supply Scheme that provides more than 1.6 million of Western Australia's two million people with their drinking water.

The requirement to act decisively to, for example, establish new water sources, increase water recycling, change water use attitudes and behaviours, and catchment management initiatives to harvest more water, suddenly took on a new urgency. No longer was water use efficiency and genuine conservation a nice concept. It had become a 'must have' fact of life.

A further driver was the fact that, unlike the big eastern states cities of Sydney, Melbourne and Brisbane and some major provincial cities, the 1.6 million users of the Integrated Water Supply Scheme – taking in Perth, some parts of the south-west and out to Kalgoorlie-Boulder through the Goldfields pipeline – were inconvenienced only by a roster limiting the use of water sprinkler systems to two days a week. This two-day roster stood in stark contrast to Melbourne and Sydney where complete bans on outside watering were frequently in place during early 2000s.

In brief – Perth has stayed green – and the government and the Water Corporation is determined that this happy state of affairs remains!

In many ways the Perth Seawater Desalination Plant, built on a critical timeframe to be providing 45 gigalitres a year of new water into the IWSS from November 2006 – and in the process becoming the Scheme's single biggest water supply source – was the lightning rod for the Water Corporation's Security through Diversity program to secure the state's water future.

Essentially the long-term program, which was clearly defined and under way in the early 2000s, involves a combination of the development of new groundwater and surface water sources, improved catchment management, major (and increasingly innovative) water recycling, ongoing demand management initiatives, water trading with irrigators in the south-west of WA, and seawater desalination.

Jim Gill, who has been in charge of the Water Corporation since it began in 1996, is in no doubt of the utility's most memorable achievements in its first 10 years. He points to a source development program that doubled water into the Integrated Scheme, then a fast-track program to help overcome the devastating effects of the worst drought in WA's history. He then talks of the Corporation's role in a range of water efficiency programs that lead the nation and, on a major scale, the implementation of the Security through Diversity program.

Dr Gill acknowledges the critical role of the Corporation as a leading player in the infrastructure development of Western Australia but says this is expected of an organisation charged with providing the state with the vast majority of its water services.

However, he believes the response and rock solid plans to combat the threat of the drying climate is what, in future years, the Corporation and its people will be remembered for, and what will continue to immortalise it in the history of the state's development.

"There is no doubt that the drying climate is one of the most critical issues Western Australia has faced," he says. "We do not know when the dramatic decline in the stream flows to our dams, that has reduced run-off in the past 30 years by two thirds, will end – if it ends at all. As climates and environments change, the timing of sustainable new water source developments and the ability of the community to adopt water efficient behaviours is imperative.

"The Water Corporation will continue to play a lead role in providing a more secure water future for WA. Initiatives like industrial water recycling at the Kwinana Water Reclamation Plant, the Perth Seawater Desalination Plant, the aggressive pursuit of water trading and the exploration of major new groundwater sources, provide the high profile proof that this is the case.

In the background, many other initiatives including a range of waterwise community initiatives are being pursued, perhaps less spectacularly, but nevertheless equally as innovative and necessary."

Dr Gill said there was no doubt that the approach adopted by the Water Corporation, on behalf of the Western Australian government and community, of diversifying its sources of water to minimise the risk and uncertainty associated with climate change puts it at the forefront of urban water management in Australia and internationally.

"Other cities throughout Australia and overseas are adopting and will continue to adopt measures to deal with limited water supply, but I doubt I would get to many arguments in the Australian water industry when I say that no one is tackling this challenge in such a holistic and integrated manner as WA's Water Corporation," he says.

"While our organisation is only 10 years old we draw on more than 100 years of history so in that sense we are not a rising star. But, I believe we have the programs in place to say that we are a star performer, under very difficult circumstances, in the delivery of a product that is more precious than gold."

Above: Mundaring Weir – starting point for the Goldfields Pipeline.

SALLY MALAY MINING LIMITED

Sally Malay is proof that Western Australia is indeed a land of opportunity for those willing to give business a go.

Sally Malay Mining Limited was founded in 2001 by its managing director, Peter Harold, and a group of private investors, with the primary focus of bringing its namesake mineral resource, the Sally Malay nickel sulphide orebody, into production as quickly as possible and using the cashflow from that asset to build a significant Australian mining house.

In just five years the company has already surpassed it original goal and is now operating two underground nickel mines in Western Australia, employing more than 200 people with a forecast production for 2005/06 of over 10,000 tonnes contained nickel.

Over that short period the company has grown from a market capitalisation of $12 million at the time of its original public offering to be included in the ASX /S&P 300 Index with a capitalisation of over $150 million. With both operations ramping up to full production in 2006, the company is on track to generate in excess of $150 million in revenue and a profit of over $15 million in 2005/06 and strong revenues and profits thereafter.

The company's main assets are the Sally Malay Project, 240km south of Kununurra in the East Kimberley region of Western Australia and the Lanfranchi Joint Venture, 40km south of Kambalda in the Eastern Goldfields.

The Sally Malay orebody was discovered in the 1970s and had a number of owners before the company acquired it in early 2001. A bankable feasibility study was commenced immediately and delivered in July 2002, incorporating a resource of over 65,000 tonnes nickel, 27,000 tonnes copper and 3,400 tonnes cobalt.

Financing and marketing was completed during 2002 and the $65 million project development commenced in early 2003. The development consisted of the construction of a 750,000 tonne per annum mineral processing plant and associated infrastructure including a 200 person accommodation village, process water and tailings dams, power station and open pit mining operation.

The plant treats the Sally Malay ore using a conventional crushing, grinding and flotation circuit to produce a high quality nickel/copper/cobalt concentrate which is trucked to Wyndham and shipped to China for smelting. The plant was commissioned in August 2004 and has since outperformed its design parameters in terms of throughput and metallurgical recoveries. The operation produces over 8,000 tonnes per annum of nickel in concentrate plus copper and cobalt credits and based on the current reported resource will operate until at least 2009. The open pit mine ceased operations in January 2006 and all ore is now sourced from underground via a decline at a rate of 600,000 tonnes per annum.

There are other known sulphide mineral occurrences in the Kimberley in close proximity to the Sally Malay plant, including the Sally Malay Deeps (below the 500m fault which is the limit of the existing Sally Malay orebody) and the company is confident that operations will continue well after 2009, treating ore from its own tenements, joint venture ground and/or 3rd party feeds.

In essence the company has the only sulphide processing plant in the Kimberley region and is well placed to leverage from this commercial advantage to maximise the profitability of this asset for many years to come.

In late 2004, the company purchased a 75 percent interest in the Lanfranchi Joint Venture from Nickel West (formerly WMC Resources), which included a package of mineral licences containing over 74,000 tonnes of nickel in resource. WMC Resources mined over 100,000 tonnes of nickel in sulphide from the Lanfranchi tenements over a 15-year period from underground. The ore was processed through its own concentrator, 42km to the north on the outskirts of Kambalda.

Right: Aerial view of Sally Malay Processing Plant.

Sally Malay is the majority owner and operator of the Lanfranchi Joint Venture and immediately after the purchase commenced rehabilitation of the decline and underground infrastructure and re-commenced mining on a limited scale in January 2004 on the Lanfranchi orebody itself, using hand held mining techniques.

The company then focused its efforts on developing the decline access to the high grade Helmut South orebody, with production ramping up to in excess of 10,000 tonnes per month in March 2006. The joint venture installed a paste fill plant, which was commissioned in early 2006, to better manage the ground conditions and allow higher extraction rates to be achieved.

The Lanfranchi Joint Venture is forecast to produce over 2,500 tonnes contained nickel in 2005/06, ramping up to over 6,000 tonnes contained nickel in 2006/07. In addition, the tenements are considered highly prospective for additional nickel discoveries and the joint venture has already returned positive results from limited exploration activity during 2005.

A more aggressive exploration program will commence in 2006 and the company is confident significant additional mineralisation will be discovered on the joint venture tenements. Nickel West is contracted to take up to 350,000 tonnes ore per annum from the Lanfranchi Joint Venture, which will allow the joint venture to expand production significantly if it can identify and develop additional resources.

Sally Malay is a young company, run by young and enthusiastic people with a vision to grow the business. The company is extremely well placed to leverage its current operations to achieve its ultimate goal of building a significant mining house.

Above: Underground operations at Sally Malay. Top: Sally Malay open pit.

WESTERN AUSTRALIAN LOCAL GOVERNMENT ASSOCIATION

The powerful and influential Western Australian Local Government Association represents and leads WA's 144 councils.

There are few WA industries with the size and diversity of local government and consequently, the opportunities, says WALGA president Bill Mitchell.

"As the peak body created by local governments to represent their collective interests, the association is ideally placed to harness the collective buying power of WA local governments to produce better results for all," he said.

"This extends to being a source for information, services and products to assist member councils realise their full potential."

The association provides representation on issues affecting the sector, regularly meeting relevant state government ministers and department heads, as well as industry and business leaders. It also manages grant-funded programs including RoadWise, Municipal Waste Advisory Council, Perth Biodiversity Project, Linking Councils and Communities and the federal government's Natural Resource Management program.

WALGA is an independent, private entity, not a government agency or department. A membership-based organisation, it is funded via member subscriptions, negotiated business agreements and government grants.

WALGA is governed by a president and state council of 24 zone representatives of elected members.

Association chief executive Ricky Burges said WALGA existed to enhance the capacity and build a positive public profile for local government, as well as represent and lead it.

Cr Mitchell said the association had a vision of two key principles underpinning WA local government.

"That councils be built on good governance, autonomy, local leadership, democracy, community engagement and diversity," he said.

"And, that they have the capacity to provide economically, socially and environmentally sustainable services and infrastructure that meet the needs of their communities."

Cr Mitchell said last year, results of independent research found that local government was the most trusted of the three spheres of government.

"A statewide survey ranked local government highest for trust at more than twice the rate of the state government (ranked second) and the federal government (ranked third)," he said.

Cr Mitchell said WALGA was a new organisation with a long history.

"It was launched in its current form in 2001 but its beginnings date back more than 100 years," he said.

"The current association formed from the merger of four organisations that used to represent the sector."

It took more than a decade of negotiations to bring the Local Government Association, the Country Shire Councils' Association, the Country Urban Councils' Association and the WA Municipal Association together.

The WA Municipal Association, formed in 1989, was the first umbrella organisation for the other three.

"The merger of the four organisations was to provide a truly representative and united voice for local government in WA," Cr Mitchell said.

WALGA now represents about 1,350 elected members and more than 12,000 employees who serve the almost 2 million constituents in WA's 144 councils. Those local governments' areas range in size from the 1.5km² Shire of Peppermint Grove to the 371,696 km² Shire of East Pilbara.

Below right: WALGA President Cr Bill Mitchell and CEO Ricky Burges.
Below: WALGA head office is Local Government House in West Perth.

"The total local government operating revenue in WA is almost $1.8 billion, with 45 percent of council income provided by rates," Cr Mitchell explained.

"In terms of operating revenue, the City of Stirling manages the largest budget of $122 million, while a number of councils have budgets less than $2 million."

The association employs about 70 staff, most in its head office in West Perth.

"We have two distinct areas of operation – developing and reviewing policy positions for local government and providing operational services," Cr Mitchell said.

"Policy teams work in six key areas – community, development, environment, governance, transport and waste management.

"The services division provides a complementary suite of quality, value-for-money services dedicated to the needs of local governments."

Cr Mitchell said one of the association's core functions was to negotiate agreements through its commercial services program to result in savings to members.

"The association also provides human resource and industrial relations services through Workplace Solutions and risk management and insurance services in partnership with the Local Government Insurance Service," he said.

"Our vision is to be powerful and influential in representing, supporting and leading local government."

Above: About 900 delegates from across the state attend Local Government Week organised by WALGA.
Top: Celebrations in 2005 for the 10th anniversary of one of WALGA's key partnerships the Local Government Insurance Service.

ARMADALE REDEVELOPMENT AUTHORITY

The Armadale Redevelopment Authority is an organisation with a vision. Over the next decade, WA's largest state government urban renewal project will be the catalyst for the rapid development and growth of the Armadale and Kelmscott town centres, as well as large residential and industrial areas nearby.

The ARA manages the redevelopment of eight discrete sites covering about 2,000 hectares of previously under-used, mostly privately owned land.

ARA chairman Gerry Gauntlett said each site had strategic attributes that would contribute to Armadale's future social and economic growth.

Mr Gauntlett said that the ARA, a WA Government Planning and Infrastructure agency, started work in March 2002 and quickly established itself as an innovative business and community leader.

Unlike other WA redevelopment authorities, the ARA's scheme areas (over which it has planning and development control) are predominantly privately owned so its focus is to facilitate business and community growth through investment, sponsorship and civic works.

Mr Gauntlett said the ARA worked closely with local MLA and planning and infrastructure minister Alannah MacTiernan, the City of Armadale, community groups and businesses to identify new infrastructure needed to restore Armadale as a strategic regional centre.

A key characteristic of the Armadale area is its fragile water environment.

As a result, the ARA is the first WA regulatory authority to require all developments to pass a sustainability audit.

"We have developed our own web-based tool that assesses the sustainability components of proposed developments," Mr Gauntlett said.

"Factors include efficiency of land, water and energy use, environmental and visual impact, waste management, access and security."

The ARA's residential estate at Champion Drive is the first in the Perth metropolitan area where installation of rainwater tanks is a condition of building approval.

The authority's commitment to sustainability also led it to establish a partnership with the CSIRO to develop state-of-the-art water management practices at its biggest residential development, Brookdale.

Brookdale is one of two Australian pilot projects chosen for the CSIRO's Water for a Healthy Country research program, which aims to achieve the first total urban water management outcome in WA.

"Brookdale will be a distinctive residential area developed over 15 to 20 years for up to 30,000 people," Mr Gauntlett said.

"It will showcase industry best practice in sustainable urban development – including resource management, water-sensitive design and energy-efficient housing."

Another high-profile ARA project is Champion Lakes, an exciting recreational park and international-standard rowing, canoeing and triathlon complex. The ARA took advantage of the extension of Tonkin Highway to excavate a 2.2km rowing course (which provided fill for the highway construction). The course was then lined with high-density plastic.

Champion Lakes is filled with non-potable water from a 700m deep bore in the Yarragadee aquifer, which began flowing in May, 2005, and reached design level in January, 2006. It holds 2.8 gigalitres – the equivalent of 100,000 Olympic-size swimming pools.

Other plans for Champion Lakes include an Aboriginal Interpretative and Enterprise Centre, resort-style accommodation, a high-quality residential area, conference facilities and small-scale business and commercial activities.

"A series of habitat islands will have wading, nesting and roosting zones for birds," Mr Gauntlett said. "There will also be passive recreation areas

Right: The annual Armadale Fiesta is a summer highlight.

and pedestrian paths, including boardwalks to the conservation zones."

A 26ha residential estate of 400 high-quality single and grouped housing units on the southern corner of the Champion Lakes site will provide more housing diversity in the area.

"This development also continues the theme of demonstrating best practice in energy and water efficiency," he said.

Mr Gauntlett said $140 million invested in expanding shopping centres in Armadale's city centre was evidence of renewed economic vigour in the area.

Other local projects include the ARA-initiated bid for an Australian Technical College for Armadale, a major education precinct adjacent to the new rail station and a high-density residential development on the western side of the railway.

"That residential development will support the government's transit-oriented development policy," he said.

The Kelmscott town centre is undergoing a major makeover that includes a new public plaza, redeveloped rail station, civic and commercial buildings and medium-density residential development.

"The ARA plan integrates the centre, east and west of Albany Highway,

improves the entire shopping precinct and increases traffic safety," Mr Gauntlett said. Adjacent areas will also benefit from development.

In Forrestdale, about 188ha of under-used land will be transformed into a business park, a new focus of economic and employment activity that will have the potential to generate up to 5,000 new jobs.

Mr Gauntlett said the catalyst for the Forrestdale Business Park was a developer contribution scheme, which required landowners to contribute to roads and services pre-funded by the ARA.

"The park is linked to all major transport routes, bordered by the Tonkin Highway extension to the west, Armadale Road and Ranford Road," he said.

"Planned as WA's first major sustainable industrial area, Forrestdale Business Park will use innovative water management practices to cut costs and reduce impact on the environment.

"Other sustainability practices include resource sharing, recycling to make the most of materials and energy and establishing links between businesses to encourage use of industrial by-products."

These ambitious projects will enhance the potential of the diverse Armadale-Kelmscott area with its strong character and identity.

CALIBRE PROJECTS

Among the brightest rising stars on the West Australian business scene is engineering consulting group Calibre Projects.

The firm entered the resource sector four years ago and the timing could not have been sweeter, with the state's current minerals boom generating much of Calibre's present workload and helping it grow its workforce from an initial 15 staff members in 2002 to more than 450 today.

The pace of growth was so rapid the company was recently ranked Perth's fastest growing private company in the *WA Business News* Rising Stars survey.

And there is more to come, according to Calibre co-founder and managing director Jack Rowley.

"We are confident that in the next couple of years we will again double the size of our business," Mr Rowley said.

Mr Rowley set up the business with Ray Munro and Dave Walker in the very early stages of the minerals boom. The partners have vast experience in the iron ore industry and could sense the makings of an enormous business opportunity.

"We felt it was the perfect time to invest in a company and build on our personal reputations," Mr Rowley said.

Below: Hamersley Iron Yandi Stockyard.

"If anything, we underestimated the appetite for iron ore from the growing Chinese market, which is the main reason we have been able to experience such successful growth."

What began as a small quality project management and engineering service provider to the Australian resource industry has since expanded on a global scale.

Calibre's core business is engineering, procurement and construction management services to the mining sector. It has worked on some of Rio Tinto's major expansion projects in the Pilbara, including the Yandi and Eastern Range mine expansions, the West Angelas upgrade and expansion of the rail infrastructure.

But while these projects have kept the company busy, Calibre has always been mindful of the need to grow. Its management has been working on a long-term plan, beyond the current iron ore boom which has necessitated the adoption of quality systems and process management under the umbrella of the Australian Business Excellence Framework. In fact, Calibre is one of the few service companies in Australia to be triple-accredited in quality, safety and environment as a result of the initiative.

The company has also received certification by SAI Global in Environment Management Systems to AS/NZS ISO 14001-2004 which provides a framework for managing environmental responsibilities and integrating them into overall business operations.

"We've certainly built a very solid platform to ensure the sustainability of the business. We're here for the long term," Mr Rowley said.

The company's strategy is to diversify its operations into new industry sectors like oil and gas, nickel and chemicals and new geographic areas.

Calibre expanded its reach in 2005, opening offices in Melbourne, Adelaide and Singapore and was awarded its first international contract later that year with BHP Billiton's Maruwai Coal project in Indonesia.

"2005 was remarkable for the Calibre group of companies. We set out to achieve growth, diversification and strengthening of our corporate systems and we exceeded our expectations," Mr Rowley said.

The diversification strategy has led to the formation of five business divisions. Calibre Projects is focused on project delivery and engineering services; Calibre Controls provides automation and process control services; Calibre Systems delivers system and information technology management; Calibre Safety Services specialises in training and consulting; and Calibre Rail delivers heavy haulage rail engineering services.

All divisions provide complementary services and allow the Calibre group to attract clients in new geographic locations and industries.

"Our efforts to diversify into new industry sectors and locations were supported by our appointment as the study manager for the Maruwai project which gives us a foothold in the coal sector and secures our relationship with BHP Billiton, one of the world's biggest miners," Mr Rowley said.

The company is also looking to capitalise on India's growing status as a major iron ore exporter over the next decade.

"Market research tells us that India could be the next Pilbara," Mr Rowley said.

While the company enjoys good fortunes on the business front, it is also mindful of its role as an active member in the WA community. It maintains a strong philanthropic presence in Perth, led primarily by its support of Youth Focus, a community organisation working with young people and Curtin University's engineering faculty, where a common room for senior students has been built. It also supports the Cancer Council's annual Relay for Life and the Princess Margaret-Youth Focus Allendale Abseil.

The company has also taken a keen interest in local and regional sports, offering financial and moral support to the University of Western Australia's fencing club, the Fortescue Football League, the Calibre Cockatoos' international water polo team and the South Augusta Cricket Club.

Culturally, Calibre became an Orchestral Partner with the West Australian Symphony Orchestra for the 2005-2006 season. The partnership includes the sponsorship of the orchestra's Principal Percussionist and resulted in the company's achievement of the Western Australian state Arts Sponsorship Scheme Award.

Above: Environmental management. Top: Engineering designers at work.

Having enjoyed tremendous success in its fledgling years, Calibre now has its sights set firmly on future growth.

"There is no time for complacency," Mr Rowley said.

"We are determined to remain focused on our business fundamentals – adding exceptional value to our clients and striving for commercial and technical innovation.

"We now intend to expand our geographic and vertical markets and deliver successful project outcomes to a wider array of clients."

LEASE EQUITY

Lease Equity is one of Western Australia's greatest business stories in the making. Established in 2002, the retail property consultants have already joined the ranks of Australia's industry leaders undertaking multiple transactions across the country.

Some of Australia's leading property owners have recognised the consultancy service as an ideal asset management partner.

Companies such as AMP, Coles Myer, Deutsche Bank, Elderslie Group, ISPT, Multiplex, the Perron Group and Woolworths have all entrusted Lease Equity to manage and increase the value of their property assets.

Despite the short time it has been operating, the consultancy has achieved outstanding results for their clients.

These include the successful leasing and development of the Whitford City Shopping Centre, with a $100 million upgrade and 120 new shops; and a $26 million acquisition of Plaza Arcade which has since been redeveloped and upgraded for a further $5 million.

Lease Equity also redeveloped and extended Livingston Marketplace to include Big W and an additional 35 shops, costing more than $10 million. It then redeveloped the Village Green Shopping Centre to more than 14,500sqm of retail space for approximately $22 million.

In Perth's northern suburbs, the company redeveloped and extended the Ocean Keys Shopping Centre to include a K-Mart, Woolworths and 30 specialty shops for approximately $12 million.

Lease Equity has also redeveloped seven neighbourhood shopping centres including several national supermarket chains and specialty retailers valued at more than $50 million.

Thanks to Lease Equity, more than $20 million in annual rental is being achieved on behalf of clients throughout the Perth CBD malls.

Lease Equity works closely with its clients to quickly recognise and adapt to their changing needs.

This close relationship means the consultants can achieve the best outcome and apply the right solutions no matter what challenges the market may impose, according to Lease Equity marketing director Jim Tsagalis.

Right: Brooks Gardens Shopping Centre, Albany, Western Australia – a $45 million development. (below) Village Green Shopping Centre, Karawarra – a $21 million development.

"Our philosophy is that the advice and work we provide can always be measured in the value we help create for our clients," Mr Tsagalis said.

The business specialises in adding value to property by undertaking rigorous asset management. This is overseen by a diligent and highly educated property team.

In fact, Lease Equity's strength is in its people. The company has more than 20 outstanding employees who are in tune with every client need.

"They are the best of the best in the investment property industry," Mr Tsagalis said.

Many among the Lease Equity's staff are leaders in their profession and are regularly being asked to lecture and help educate the industry on their cutting edge practices.

Since its inception just four years ago, the business has grown into one of Australia's leading retail property organisations.

DEPARTMENT OF INDUSTRY AND RESOURCES

Western Australia is thriving. The state is leading Australia's development with resources, research and technology, ship-building and business appeal adding to its attraction as a highly desirable place to live.

State resource projects on the drawing boards or committed are valued at nearly $60 billion. The projects will result in more than 30,000 construction jobs and more than 8,000 permanent positions.

The biggest are BHP Billiton's $1.8 billion Ravensthorpe nickel development and its $4.2 billion iron ore expansion plans in the Pilbara; Rio Tinto-led consortia plans for $4 billion iron ore expansions and FMG's proposed $2.4 billion developments.

Add to that WA's strong housing market which has refused to reflect trends in the rest of Australia and continues to reach record prices; an influx of migrants in response to a state-wide need for skilled workers and a determined effort by the WA government to address WA's infrastructure needs and the state's future looks promising.

Western Australia's lifestyle attractions range from beaches described as the best in the world, to fine vineyards producing world-renowned wines, enhanced by a Mediterranean climate that is the envy of the nation.

In the state's capital, Perth, median house prices rose through the $300,000 level in 2005, representing a 21 percent jump driven by strong economic growth, the new jobs available and the affordability of real estate compared with other Australian states.

The growth in real estate was also strong in regional areas, backed by strength in both the resources and agricultural sectors.

Strong global demand for clean energy is driving rapid expansion of the liquefied natural gas industry.

Leading the way are projects such as the Chevron/Shell and Exxon-Mobil $11 billion Gorgon gas/condensate project, with processing plans centred on Barrow Island.

BHP Billiton is also looking to develop an LNG plant at Onslow at a cost of $4 billion, while Woodside's Pluto LNG plant, on the North-West Shelf, is forecast to cost about $5 billion.

The services sector, which accounts for about 70 percent of the state's economic activity, is also highly competitive in areas such as education, health and biotechnology, building and construction, information technology and engineering.

Western Australia was described by a prominent national economic firm in late 2005 as a "pipeline to prosperity". With its domestic economic growth rate continually among the highest in the nation, it has healthy budget surpluses and low debt levels.

The state benefits from its proximity to crucial markets – Japan, China, Korea and India. Being in a similar time zone also assists financiers, both in Perth and Asian countries.

Crucial to the accelerating growth is the role of the Department of Industry and Resources, which is helping clients work more effectively with the government.

DoIR also provides advice through a network of overseas trade and investment offices in China, Europe, India, Indonesia, Japan, Malaysia, the Middle East, South Korea, Taiwan, Thailand and the United States.

Above: Department of Industry and Resources director general, Mr Jim Limerick.

Its focus is to broaden the state's economic basis, while ensuring that development is responsible and, importantly, sustainable.

Western Australia's industrial growth is a result of an outwardly-focussed business culture. Through a long history of exporting a diverse range of value-added goods and services, businesses in the state know how to compete with the world's best.

An example of this is the success of the state's expanding marine and defence industry sector.

Major shipbuilding companies include Austal, Tenix and the Australian Submarine Corporation which are complemented by a range of smaller builders and subcontractors. WA is also pioneering the aluminium ferry industry – leading the world in this technology and providing 25 percent of the world's high speed lightweight ferries.

These vessels are produced in the 15 to 30-metre range catering for a diverse range of users including vehicle and troop transport.

Another development is the establishment of major companies in Perth, such as Raytheon which is working on a new combat system for the Collins-class submarines all of which are based in Western Australia.

Many oil and gas companies have also based their offices in Perth, to the point where the main thoroughfare – St Georges Terrace – has been nicknamed "Houston on the Terrace".

Biotechnology is also a growing component of the state's commercial world. One of the most prominent examples is Clinical Cell Culture, the result of research at the Royal Perth Hospital and founded by the 2005 Australian of the Year, Dr Fiona Wood.

Biotechnology represented 10 percent of new firms in Australia in 2005 and DoIR estimates more than 140 biotech companies and organisations are active in WA with 45 core firms employing 542 people.

Some of these firms are based at a world-class technology park at Bentley in Perth's southern suburbs. The park provides an important catalyst for science and technology development, including research, information and communications technology, resources and energy, environment and education.

DoIR also offers assistance to prospective skilled migrants, aids the development of regional business, promotes West Australian products, supports the economic independence of Aboriginal people through its Office of Aboriginal Economic Development and attracts investment to industry sectors, including manufacturing.

But, bold facts about economics aside, it is the lifestyle which attracts people to Western Australia and keeps them here. In 2005, Esperance beaches were voted the best in Australia.

The local crayfish industry, worth about $265 million a year, combined with marron, yabbies and fish, and the world-class wines from the Swan Valley, South-West and Mount Barker regions, entice the palate.

Western Australia's attractions and the many opportunities it offers keep West Aussies, investors and visitors coming back for more.

Above: Western Australia is one of the world's major iron ore producers. As the state's premier commodity sector, iron ore accounts for about 30 percent of WA's mineral sales. PHOTO COURTESY OF PILBARA IRON

Left: Western Australia is recognised globally for achievements in areas such as biomedical, agricultural and environmental biotechnology.

TECHNOLOGY PRECINCT

After 20 years in operation, WA's Technology Park is one of the state's economic success stories; home to 90 companies employing more than 2,500 people and producing a combined turnover of $500 million per annum.

But the new millennium necessitates new strategies and the stage is being set for growth of an entirely different manner.

Following the success of Technology Park the original concept is being expanded to incorporate adjacent organizations and communities to inspire innovation, excellence and cross fertilization between disciplines.

This combination of virtual and physical networks is known as the Technology Precinct of Western Australia.

The concept for the Precinct has taken its cue from the brilliant discourse on 'fractals', by renowned twentieth century mathematician Benoit Mandelbrot.

Fractal geometry is a mathematical language devised to describe irregular and fragmented patterns in nature. At the heart of the language is the discovery that the closer one examines a part of the pattern the more it mirrors the whole.

The Precinct then will be a self-referential pattern, which when magnified again and again, always resembles the original. It is this pattern of growth that will define the Precinct by replicating innovation on all levels, through dialogue, collaboration and product development.

To help create this pattern its foundation will be built upon four 'communities of interest'.

These communities, hinged upon the themes of education, enterprise, research and community, act as rallying points for the Precinct's constituents. Furthermore, they will provide forums for those with similar goals to meet, converse and socialise.

The Precinct itself consists of an area that has a wealth of facilities and a diverse range of organisations.

These include research and development organisations, manufacturing industries, government departments, educational facilities, at all levels, recreational facilities and social and community organisations.

Complementing this is the surrounding residential community, largely composed of the aged and students.

The core opportunity for the Precinct will be to generate synergies within and between these communities, which in turn will hinge upon the development of social capital.

Broadly defined, this is the value of social networks – friendships, family and community organisations – they are drivers of productivity, well-being and sustainability within our communities.

"Buoying commercial ventures and research initiatives will be some of the more obvious by-products of this social capital creation," says chair of the Technology Precinct Board Marian Tye.

"But perhaps more importantly, by developing social capital within the Precinct, the community will be generating more than excellence in the various fields represented here already, they will all be nurturing a rich culture of social networks."

The Board believes that in this way the Precinct will not only be identified for its innovative commercial, education and research achievements, but also for its strong community ethos.

"And it's this ethos that will help retain and attract skilled community members, both domestically and internationally," Ms Tye adds.

At first look, the entities of the Precinct are seemingly disparate. But although different, they hold key values in common, such as sharing, collaboration, integrity, ethics and innovation and entrepreneurship.

These values define two distinctive elements of the Precinct: 'ethical innovation' and "bringing things to reality."

The philosophical foundation for the Precinct's social planning is being developed by local consultancy Creating Communities.

"The new approach to how to solve these issues of justice and equity is built around the concept of sustainable growth, which is progress that supports social, environmental and economic assets," explains company director Donna Shepherd.

"A prerequisite of sustainable growth is ethical innovation, as it suggests consideration of all possible social, environmental and economic impacts, and as such is a starting point for sustainable growth.

"By positioning itself as a leader in ethical innovation, the Precinct can capitalise on the tremendous investment that's now going into solving how best to share and grow these assets.

To help bring the concept to the next stage, the state government has committed $8.5 million to implement the capital infrastructure of the master plan's stage 1.

Spearheaded by the WA Department of Industry and Resources (DoIR), the Precinct overlaps three local governments: the City of South Perth, Town of Victoria Park and the City of Canning.

Stage 1 of the master plan includes the establishment of a joint Town Planning Scheme, which aims to create a common vision for town planning in the three localities.

In collaboration with David Lock Associates, urban design firm EPCAD has been charged with creating the master plan.

Primarily, the plan is focused on economic development and identifies strategies for a resource and energy hub, a centre for excellence in technology, a communication portal, training initiatives and industry and tertiary education compacts.

"This physical plan provides an urban framework that facilitates growth, as well as social and community interaction with linked neighbourhoods and a new activity centre designed to accommodate enhanced public transport," says EPCAD director Howard Mitchell.

"And any amendments to the statutory planning procedures will streamline the development approval process if development initiatives comply with the objectives of the Precinct."

The Precinct will offer a range of sites and development opportunities delivering employment, education and accommodation within a cohesive urban landscape that links distinct character areas.

According to the brief, the proposed urban framework, as well as the plans and guidelines, all seek to allow as much flexibility as possible, while at the same time maintaining high standards and respecting the surrounding community.

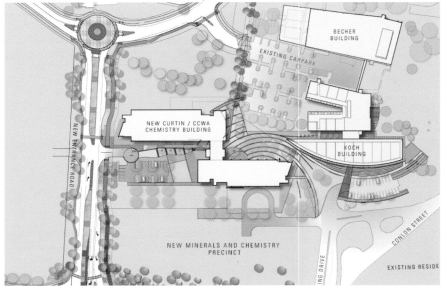

Above: Curtin University's Resources and Mineral Research and Education Precinct will be home to the biggest cluster of like-minded researchers in the southern hemisphere.

"By bringing people together through the urban form we set up the physical conditions to accommodate a critical mass of talent. Though the concept of creating synergies for the Precinct could be construed as somewhat intangible, enabling social interaction through the physical development and encouraging clustering of related institutions and business will actually mentor creativity," says Mr Mitchell.

As an example of what the future will bring, Precinct member Curtin University of Technology has already been progressing its own plans as an integral part of the master plan.

Scheduled to be built in 2008, the proposed Resources and Mineral Research and Education Precinct will be home to the biggest cluster of like-minded researchers in the southern hemisphere.

The project embraces the co-location of the state government's chemistry centre of WA, CSIRO's minerals research facilities and Curtin's department of applied chemistry to the new university site.

The Western Australian Institute of Chemical Science, as well as two mining-related Cooperative Research Centre (CRC) headquarters will also be accommodated in the same location.

The ultimate vision for the cluster will provide a seamless pathway for nearby high school students specialising in science, maths and technology through to undergraduate science, postgraduate research studies and employment.

"Australia has a once-in-a-generation opportunity to facilitate the creation of this world-class facility," says Curtin's director for research and development Tony Tate.

"The opportunity to co-locate organizations with extensive standing and reputation in research alongside tertiary teaching programs in similar science disciplines will provide a boost for the future of science within WA. While the co-location of almost 200 professional research and teaching staff will focus the world's attention on both the state and the nation."

Mr Tate further expects that such a concentration of expertise will act as an attractor for other activities, such as the relocation of related private sector organisations and business incubation.

Ms Tye agrees, saying frameworks like this seek to create a climate of excellence and innovation in which ideas, resources, people and investment are mobilised towards common goals.

"A community of this sort is achieved by creating a climate in which skills, passions and endeavor are nurtured, and cross-disciplined partnerships are forged," she said.

She adds that in contrast to the potential sterility of other business parks, the Precinct will be a vibrant, culturally diverse and innovative space that seeks to pool ideas, people and resources.

"Being able to mobilise the sum of its parts into a powerful collective means we will reach an enviable local and international position with an exceptional reputation within research and development, as well as a variety of commercial pursuits by embodying the new economy of ideas, innovation and collaboration," she said.

Within such a dynamic space accidental synergies are common place. Within a space in which ideas and people move freely random synergies evolve with increasing frequency. Consequently, innovation becomes the norm rather than the exception.

"Intellectual and social networks of this sort elevate the reputation of the Precinct as a place of imaginative solutions and new industry benchmarks in the international marketplace," says Ms Tye.

The Precinct already has in place access to a Global Alliance Centre (GAC) for visiting science and technology managers.

This is a 'hotdesk' facility that allows international visitors to continue with their business and carry out strategic and business activities.

The GAC will assist in creating strategic linkages between tenants of other science and technology parks in different locations. In addition, it will help strengthen the network of global science and technology managers and will provide a medium for information and knowledge sharing on current trends and future directions.

"The innovation and networks of this Precinct will create cross-disciplinary interactions that spark innovation, and in turn create opportunities for problem solving," explains Ms Tye.

"From this simple bringing together of different disciplines we'll attract more research funds and investment. The most successful urban places have one thing in common — something distinctive that attracts both people and investment.

"It can be a building, a festival, a cultural experience, a hub of excellence or a combination of diverse experiences. Whatever the ingredients, the success of local economies and the vibrancy of places is dependant on it."

The challenge for the Technology Precinct is not the need to invent a distinctive asset to give the area a competitive advantage. The entities associated with the Precinct, both individually and collectively, already have distinctive elements on which to draw.

The challenge is to clearly define how to articulate this distinctiveness into a clear and compelling message that generates excitement and attracts business, both now and in the future.

An invitation is extended to like-minded people to share the future with Technology Precinct, Western Australia.

AZURE CAPITAL

The booming economy of Western Australia is prompting organisations from all walks of life to make the most from their hard-earned dollars.

But finding the best advice on maximising investment opportunities is not as easy as walking into one of the large financial institutions.

In fact, for many smaller investors, the big banks offer little flexibility – they simply consider them too small.

Azure Capital is a boutique investment bank in Perth which caters to smaller clients, offering a personalised service tailored to the needs of individual clients.

The story of Azure Capital began in 2004. Its founders, John Poynton, Mark Barnaba, Geoff Rasmussen, Ben Lisle and Simon Price are still closely involved with the firm, which is based at the Exchange Plaza in the heart of the city.

The firm has 17 full-time staff in Perth, including the five directors, three managers, five associates and four support staff. In addition, Tait Farrow Azure – the company's wealth management affiliate which shares office space with the firm – has three full-time staff.

Below: (from left to right) Mark Barnaba, Simon Price, Geoff Rasmussen, John Poynton and Ben Lisle.

"Azure Capital is a boutique merchant bank providing financial advisory services in the areas of equity capital markets, mergers and acquisitions and project finance," Mr Rasmussen said.

"Our emphasis is on serving organisations that are not well served by larger investment banks."

"We differentiate ourselves from our competitors by providing clients with access to a senior team who are 100 percent based in Perth – as opposed to some competitors who bring people in from the east."

Azure also offers a broad range of skill sets in corporate finance, law, stockbroking and management consulting. The firm has an in-depth understanding of the broader dynamics impacting on clients.

"Instead of simply executing deals, we advise clients, even if that means advising them not to do a deal if that is what we think is in their best interests," Mr Price said.

It is the company policy that at least two directors will be deeply involved in each assignment.

The company does not agree with the common practice of partners being present at the beginning and end of a project, leaving more junior employees to do all the work.

Azure's goal is to build long-term relationships with clients by being a trusted adviser. It wants the clients to feel confident they can turn to Azure to help solve their most difficult strategic and corporate issues and assist in the successful execution of the critical transactions that shape their business.

The firm also has strong links to the national and international capital markets with a broad network of contacts across a range of investment funds and intermediaries.

Azure has great contacts in the business community, which stems from the background and caliber of its people. For example, Mr Poynton is the chairman-elect of Alinta Limited and a director of many other companies including Multiplex and Burswood, giving him a lot of exposure to the wider business community.

"What makes our firm special is that we work as a team and offer our clients the combined skill set and contact base of five experienced people, rather than being a place where five advisory practices centred on five individuals happen to share an office," Mr Price explained.

Azure's major milestones are testament to the high quality of its staff and the transactions it has undertaken.

Azure has been highly successful in building a substantial share of the West Australian merger and acquisition market, with several high profile transactions concluded or under way. These include the Consolidated Minerals acquisition of Reliance, the merger of Monarch and Siberia and the proposed merger between Home Building Society and Statewest.

The company has also worked on a range of capital raisings including the initial public offering of Little World Beverages, the initial public offering of Phylogica and project finance for the Langer Heinrich Uranium project in Namibia, owned by Paladin Resources.

"A large portion of our work has traditionally been concerned with IPOs, placements and private equity," Mr Lisle said.

"Whilst our directors have always had some involvement in listed mergers and acquisitions, in the past 12 months we have made mergers and acquisitions a particular focus and have been extremely pleased with the growth in this area of our business."

Reputation is always of paramount importance for Azure Capital. The firm is very selective in what it does and who it deals with to ensure quality is maintained at the highest level.

The ongoing commodities boom has seen a period of extremely strong growth in WA, which has provided a fantastic environment to launch the business. This growth has been accompanied by a number of corporate success stories including Wesfarmers, Woodside and Alinta, which have assisted in building the state's credibility and relevance in the eastern states and abroad.

The company and its principals have had a long involvement in the West Australian business community and are proud of the quality of its clients, the team and the firm's culture.

"We are also extremely pleased with the way we have positioned ourselves as a credible player in the West Australian investment banking sector within a relatively short period of time," Mr Lisle said.

"We now have one of the largest investment banking teams on the ground in WA with a growing track record of successfully completed transactions and an excellent pipeline of opportunities."

Azure Capital will continue to grow into a regional, mid-tier, investment bank that delivers world-class people and results for clients.

MITSUI E&P AUSTRALIA PTY LTD

*Western Australia's
rich resource fields
are proving a lure for
overseas companies
flocking to contribute to
the state's biggest
export industry.*

One newcomer to WA is an old hand in the resource investment game and hails all the way from Japan.

Mitsui E&P Australia (MEPAU) was established in the heart of Perth in 2004 but its parent company, Japanese conglomerate Mitsui & Co., has played an active role in Australia since 1909.

MEPAU is the oil and gas exploration and production arm of the Australasian region for Mitsui.

Mitsui is one of Japan's largest "trading houses", a conglomerate involved in a diverse range of businesses including oil and gas, metal products and minerals, machinery, electronics and information, chemicals, and consumer products and services.

The company has a market capitalisation of approximately 2.6 trillion yen or about $A30 billion and gross revenues of 3.5 trillion yen ($A40 billion). It is a truly global giant.

MEPAU managing director Dave Nakafuji and general manager Toru Matsui spearhead the 15-strong WA team.

Despite its relative youth, MEPAU has already secured a 40 percent stake in a joint venture with Woodside in the development of oil production in the Enfield oil project off Exmouth in WA's north. The joint venture is also progressing with an adjacent oil field development, the Vincent field.

"This is a significant investment for Mitsui and confirms its commitment as an active player in the Australian energy sector," Mr Nakafuji said.

The company also manages two affiliated companies – Wandoo Petroleum (WPP) and Mitsui E&P New Zealand (MEPNZ). Until the foundation of MEPAU, WPP had been active as the oil and gas arm of the Mitsui group since the mid 90's with an office in Sydney then in Perth. WPP, along with MEPNZ, are now managed by MEPAU as a single organisation. The three companies are involved in other oil and gas exploration, development

and production joint ventures like the Wandoo oil production in the North-West shelf, the Cliff Head oil field development offshore Dongara and the Bass Gas Project which supplies gas to the Victorian market.

In New Zealand, MEPAU is working on the Kupe Gas Project and Tui Area development in the offshore Taranaki Basin. The company is also an active explorer, mainly offshore around Australia and New Zealand.

Mr Matsui said the staff at the Perth office shared a wealth of expertise as well as international experience.

"We are fortunate to have an excellent team from varying backgrounds and areas of expertise, from geology, geophysics and engineering to accounting, political science, law and administration," Mr Matsui said.

"And the number of staff members continues to grow as our asset portfolio expands. Interestingly, in true West Australian style, our people have different cultural backgrounds, adding a healthy international flavour to the office."

The Perth office of WPP transformed into MEPAU in 2004 and started out as a 3 man shop, but is now a happy team of 15. The general management consists of managing director Makoto (Dave) Nakafuji, general manager Toru Matsui and deputy general manager Yasuchika (Maru) Maruyama.

Mr Nakafuji brings to MEPAU more than 30 years of international experience in the oil and gas sector.

Mr Matsui is due to return to Tokyo soon after a fruitful Australian career with Novus Petroleum, WPP and MEPAU. Deputy general manager Yasuchika Maruyama has been appointed to step up as the general manager.

The management team is supported by personal assistant Ros Markovich – one of MEPAU's original three staff.

The company's asset management team primarily ensures that all risks are managed and value is created in the investments. The team includes

Right: Enfield FPSO under Construction.

experienced asset managers, Jim Dowell and Mike Dworkin, who are responsible for the developments and production, and exploration manger Steve Ingarfield and geophysicist Mike Collins who are responsible for exploration. Technical assistant Nicky Turich keeps the asset team happy by providing assistance the boys require.

The finance and accounting team ensures the company's books are in order. The department is run by accounting and finance manager Wallace Fong and includes highly skilled chartered accountants Rudy Djajalaksana and Danielle Di Bartolomeo, and accounts assistant Maya Hamilton.

Business analyst Aki Terasawa works closely with Mr Maruyama who is also the company's commercial and business development manager. The duo provides the expertise to manage all commercial and contractual issues as well as developing new business strategies for the company.

Another member of the company, Daiki Sato, has been seconded to Woodside's Vincent Development Team as planning engineer.

Mr Nakafuji said he was proud of MEPAU's team spirit.

"Everyone works together to manage the various risks involved in our investments," Mr Nakafuji said.

His business principle is "trust comes first, business second", which he has instilled in the company.

MEPAU's parent company Mitsui has a long and proud history in Australia. Mitsui opened its Australian entity, Mitsui & Co. (Australia) in 1909. It now forms part of Mitsui's international network spanning 75 countries and 175 cities.

Over the years, the company's investment in Australia has grown. In the 1960s it focused on coal, in the 1970s it was iron ore, the 1980s brought expansion into gas and in the 1990s woodchip plantations. All these investments are expected to continue expanding in the coming years.

Mitsui is also committed to supporting the communities in which it is active. In Australia, it especially supports ideas that build stronger ties and promote mutual understanding and friendship between Japan and Australia.

In addition to supporting the arts — through Opera Australia and the Australian Ballet, health, and the environment, Mitsui's primary form of corporate support in Australia since 1972 has been the Mitsui Educational Foundation.

The Foundation selects students from nominated Australian universities to visit Japan for 18 days each year.

The aim is to introduce them to the Japanese culture, history, business and contemporary lifestyles, helping to develop and expand the knowledge and friendship between Australia and Japan. More than 260 students have visited Japan since the MEF was initiated. WA's Edith Cowan University participated in the program last year.

Mitsui also sponsors the West Australian Symphony Orchestra, as part of WASO's World Artist program.

MEPAU is committed to expanding its activities in the Australian and New Zealand oil and gas sector both through exploration and participation in projects.

The company's goal is to continue to grow and expand its asset portfolio.

Mr Nakafuji said it was his desire to "leave a legacy for the next generation". It is an exciting challenge but one the company is looking forward to as part of Mitsui's commitment to the Australian economy.

Above: MEPAU staff.
Top: MEPAU office entrance.

PERTH CONVENTION EXHIBITION CENTRE

The $220 million Perth Convention Exhibition Centre (Perth Centre) is Western Australia's only purpose-built convention, exhibition and meeting venue.

Its landmark opening on August 26, 2004, heralded a coming of age for Perth and Western Australia, elevating the state's business tourism sector to a new, global level.

The Perth Centre was developed between November 2001 and May 2004 and is run under a unique, public-private partnership – the first of its kind in Australia. It was constructed by Multiplex, with financial support from the WA government. It is owned by Perth-based company the Wyllie Group, through a 35-year lease arrangement, and is managed by leading Australian company Spotless.

Not only iconic in size and stature, the Perth Centre is making its mark for the local economy. As the new hub for the large-scale national and international conventions and events, it generates immense economic value and flow-on benefits for hundreds of local businesses and suppliers. It is also a sought-after location for weddings, functions and corporate events in the local Perth market.

In its first 18 months the venue welcomed more than 840,500 visitors to around 687 events, including 40 exhibitions and trade shows. Some 239 conferences and meetings were attended by more than 47,250 delegates.

Paul D'Arcy, the Perth Centre's chief executive, believes that the venue's arrival had placed WA in a strong competitive position.

"In addition to the state's highly desirable destination advantages, it now has the supporting infrastructure and services needed to compete at a national and international level," Mr D'Arcy said.

"The interest from the market to date clearly demonstrates that the industry in Australia and around the world has shifted its focus to include WA as a major player."

The Perth Centre has a strong focus on opening WA's doors to so-called 'super tourists'. As WA is classed as a 'long haul' destination, many conference delegates, or 'super tourists' stay in the state for between seven

and 10 days before or after their conference. Such visitation represents a considerable financial injection to the local economy, with research showing delegates spending (on average) around $600 per day, and often bringing their families with them.

Core geographic markets for Perth and the Perth Centre include Australia, New Zealand, the Asia Pacific region, Europe and the UK. To tap into those markets, the Perth Centre employs major marketing campaigns aimed at attracting large conventions in fields like health and medical sciences, mining, oil and gas, education, technology, communications and IT, sport and recreation, construction, agriculture and marine.

The appointment of sales representatives in Sydney and Melbourne adds further value to the Perth Centre's presence in key markets.

Unrivalled features highlight the state-of-the-art, three-level Perth Centre, which is located in the heart of Perth's CBD and caters for up to 5,000 delegates. Its major facilities include a 2,500-seat tiered auditorium, 19 specialist meeting rooms varying in size, six exhibition pavilions spanning 16,554sqm of exhibition space, and a 1,700-seat ballroom with spectacular views of Perth's famous Swan River and city.

Expansive floor-to-ceiling glass foyers on all three levels, stretching 300 metres, offer panoramic city and river views. Ideal for breaks and display areas, the foyers enable organisers to link facilities within the venue to maximise flexibility and creativity.

The Perth Centre houses some of the most advanced technical facilities and communications infrastructure in the Southern Hemisphere, and is the only convention centre in Australia to offer permanently installed accredited Wi-Fi Zone wireless internet connectivity.

The Perth Centre's central location provides a critical, direct business link to the city for delegates and organisers. Adjoining the venue is the Medina Grand Perth, offering 138 serviced apartments over six levels and

Right: Plaza.
Opposite page: (top) Ballrooms; (middle) Exhibition Pavilions; (bottom) Auditorium.

the Metro Bar and Bistro. A range of other hotels and apartments, as well as restaurants, bars, cafes, retail outlets, attractions and entertainment areas are all located within short walking distance.

But what has set the Perth Centre apart from its rivals since opening is the award-winning quality through all facets of its business. The Perth Centre has collected a host of prestigious industry awards, including the 2005 National and Western Australian Tourism Awards for Meetings & Business, the Catering Institute of Australia (WA) 2005 Gold Plate Award for Venue Caterers, the 2005 Restaurant & Catering Industry Association of Australia (WA) for Function / Convention Centre Catering, and the Kimberly-Clark Professional 2005 Golden Service Award.

Up to 500 employees, including a small full-time team of around 80 people, ensure a strong service and quality culture for every event held at the Perth Centre.

Culinary quality has become a hallmark of the Perth Centre's service delivery, with its innovative catering approach attracting a flood of accolades from across the country and the globe.

A talented team of 40 chefs is led by renowned executive chef Adrian Tobin and backed by the attentive service of the Perth Centre's slick banqueting staff. Together, they can cater for up to 5,000 people at a time.

Looking ahead, the Perth Centre has secured around 500 international, national and local events through until 2009, expected to attract in excess of two million visitors.

Mr D'Arcy said the destination was gearing up for further growth, with exciting plans underway for development of additional infrastructure in close proximity to the Perth Centre.

"The City of Perth has plans to revitalise the Swan River foreshore area directly in front of our venue, which includes plans for an additional hotel within walking distance," he said.

"This development, and expanded use of our beautiful river, will further complement Perth's ability to host major convention activities and will create a vibrant precinct for delegates and tourists, as well as for the local community."

ALLIANCE RECRUITMENT

When you are running a business in a booming economy like Western Australia, there is little time to spare.

But booming times also mean you need high quality staff to get the work done as quickly as possible. That is when professional help from Alliance Recruitment can prove indispensable.

Alliance Recruitment understands today's most successful businesses consist of high performing teams with a diverse range of qualities and attributes. It knows recognising the required capabilities and potential is the key to successful recruitment in a fast paced market.

The professional team at Alliance is trained to understand client needs. Its talent attraction, selection and retention capabilities allow the group to recruit across a broad spectrum of industries and disciplines.

Whether it is office support, customer service, marketing or finance, Alliance will work hard to find the best people for the job. The company can also recruit high quality professionals in IT&T, engineering, executive human resources and information and knowledge management.

Alliance Recruitment general manager Phil Freeman said the company considers itself to be not just a service provider but an integrated business partner, focused on helping clients achieve their goals and targets.

The company, formerly Workskills Professionals, was founded in 1993 and grew steadily to include offices in Adelaide and Melbourne. In 2003 Alliance was acquired by the ASX-listed Candle Australia, which employs 360 people nationally. As part of this national network, Alliance offers

clients all the strengths of a big player, together with the personal touch of boutique solutions delivered at a local level. It's a combination many of clients find attractive and productive.

"Our marketing phrase 'why make a ripple when you can make a wave' captures our past and future initiatives," Mr Freeman said.

"Building and maintaining strong alliances is an integral aspect of any long-term business success. From the Alliance perspective, this means effective and rewarding relationships with every client and job candidate.

"These relationships are built on integrity, mutual trust, hard work and of course, results."

Mr Freeman said a data base unique to the industry and developed in-house allows a competitive advantage in an industry where competition is always strong.

"A large part of our success is due to the quality people who have worked for us and we also retain long serving employees in key positions," he said.

"The company has never taken a step backwards and each year continues to grow.

"Having a diversity of clients across industries has seen us partner with some very successful organisations.

"We have built a great company which has come from nothing to being a major supplier in the market.

"We are proud not only of what we have achieved but how we have achieved it – through integrity."

*Below: General manager Phil Freeman.
Below right: Office support is just one of
Alliances' key areas of expertise.*

FOREST PRODUCTS COMMISSION

Somewhat hidden behind WA's booming mineral resources is a valuable and important timber industry.

Western Australia's famous jarrah timber grows nowhere else in the world, its strength, durability and visual beauty have been applied worldwide in decorative and structural uses. All of Western Australia's old growth forest has been reserved for conservation, and the Forest Products Commission is at the forefront in promoting an industry producing high quality furniture, flooring and joinery from well-managed regrowth forests.

Western Australia has also been a leader in plantation development in Australia. Over the past 15 years, the public and private sectors have established more than a quarter of a million hectares of eucalypt plantations in agricultural areas. These plantations are now providing the resource for a large woodchip industry and the potential for pulp production in the state. At the same time, they are helping to restore water quality – particularly salt levels – in our rivers and agricultural lands.

Forest Products Commission general manager Dr Paul Biggs says the new challenge is to drive a new phase of plantation development in Western Australia.

"In the next phase we need to target solid wood markets and expand beyond high-rainfall areas where water demand is already high," he said.

"We particularly need to increase the available resource of structural timber to complement the native forests and existing softwood plantations if the local industry is to grow and prosper."

To achieve its objective, the Commission is developing plans that match productive hardwood and softwood species with suitable soil and climatic conditions in the lower rainfall agricultural regions of the state. While growing trees in lower rainfall areas is a significant challenge, it is very attractive due to the other benefits that result.

"Plantations in lower rainfall regions deliver substantial triple-bottom-line outcomes," Dr Biggs said.

"They can reverse the rise in water tables that followed agricultural clearing to address one of the state's most significant environmental issues, salinity. In addition, plantations provide an opportunity for farmers to diversify their businesses and will bring processing industries and employment opportunities to regional areas.

"We are working with farmers, natural resource management groups and investors to bring the plan to fruition. Our vision is for a major plantation estate in the low rainfall agricultural zone that will deliver important environmental and regional development outcomes, and contribute to a world-class, sustainable forest products industry in Western Australia."

Far right: High value West Australian furniture made from jarrah and blackbutt.

Below: Expanding plantations into lower rainfall areas to restore water quality, income diversity and bring processing industries and employment opportunities to regional areas.

Below right: Dr Paul Biggs, general manager.

COMPANY INDEX

COMPANY NAME	CONTACT INFORMATION	PAGE NO.
Action Mining Services	www.actionminingservices.com.au	198
Antenna Business Development Agency	www.antennabda.com.au	183
AOT Consulting	www.aotconsulting.com	194
Armadale Redevelopment Authority	www.ara.wa.gov.au	218
Asgard Wealth Solutions	www.asgard.com.au	184
Azure Capital	www.azurecapital.com.au	230
BGC (Australia) Pty Ltd	www.bgc.com.au	170
Burswood Entertainment Complex	www.burswood.com.au	186
Calibre Projects	www.calibreprojects.com.au	220
City of Belmont	www.belmont.wa.gov.au	142
ComputerCORP	www.computercorp.com.au	190
Consolidated Minerals Ltd	www.consminerals.com.au	166
Creating Communities	www.creatingcommunities.com.au	202
Department of Industry and Resources	www.doir.wa.gov.au	224
Dôme Coffees Australia Pty Ltd	www.domecoffees.com.au	178
EBM Insurance Brokers	www.ebminsurance.com.au	174
Edge Employment Solutions	www.edge.org.au	180
Forest Products Commission	www.fpc.wa.gov.au	237
Fremantle Ports	www.fremantleports.com.au	140
GRD Limited	www.grd.com.au	188
HBF	www.hbf.com.au	152
Horwath Chartered Accountants	www.horwath.com.au	176
Humfrey Land Developments	www.hld.com.au	192
Hydramet Australia	www.hydramet.com.au	196
Jackson McDonald	www.jacmac.com.au	146
JMG	www.jmg.com.au	182
Lease Equity	www.lease-equity.com.au	222
Lionel Samson & Son	www.lionelsamson.com.au	134
Lotterywest	www.lotterywest.wa.gov.au	150
Marketforce	www.marketforce.com.au	172
Mitsui E&P Australia Pty Ltd	www.mitsui.com.au/mepau	232
Mitsui Iron Ore Development	www.mitsui.com.au	168
Perth Convention Exhibition Centre	www.perthcentre.com.au	234
Plantagenet Wines	www.plantagenetwines.com	135
RSM Bird Cameron	www.rsmi.com.au	148
Sadleirs International	www.sadleirs.com.au/international.php	137
Sadleirs Transport	www.sadleirs.com.au	136
Sally Malay Mining Ltd	www.sallymalay.com	214
Skywest Airlines	www.skywest.com.au	162
Technology Precinct	www.techparkwa.org.au/index.shtml	226
Town of Victoria Park	www.vicpark.wa.gov.au	206
The City of Perth	www.cityofperth.wa.gov.au	132
The Dowerin GWN Machinery Field Days	www.dowerinfielddays.com.au	164
The Swan Brewery	www.lion-nathan.com.au	138
WA Business News	www.wabusinessnews.com.au	204
Water Corporation	www.watercorporation.com.au	210
Western Australian Local Government Association	www.walga.asn.au	216
Westnet	www.westnet.com.au	208
Westralia Airports Corporation– Perth Airport	www.perthairport.com	154
Woodside	www.woodside.com.au	156
Wray & Associates	www.wray.com.au	144

CONTRIBUTING PHOTOGRAPHERS

Tim Acker	tim@tracker.net.au
Paul Amyes	amyes@bigpond.com
Frances Andrijich	www.andrijich.com.au
Gary Blinco	blincophotography@westnet.com.au
Alex Bond	www.alexbond.com.au
Shelly Boston	s_boston@hotmail.com
Rowan Butler	rowan@vintagered.org
Jasmin Castillo	0400 216 185
Karen Castle	kcastle@wantree.com.au
Glen Cowans	www.glencowans.com
Andrew Cutten	mining.photography@amnet.net.au
Brad Davidson	www.davidsonimagery.com
Jon Davison	www.eyeinthesky.com.au
Andrew Davoll	davoll@arach.net.au
Marcel C de Jong	www.pbase.com/mdejong
Craig Dobson	kimproduce@bigpond.com
Wendy D'Souza	www.wdsphotography.com
Ben Fleay	benf_108@hotmail.com
Christian Fletcher	www.christianfletcher.com.au
Jenny Fletcher	www.christianfletcher.com.au
Richard Gale	0419 844 257
Matt Galligan	www.mattgalligan.com.au
Richard Giles	richard.giles@gmail.com
Matthew Goddard-Jones	matt@eggdesign.com.au
Albert Gunawan	albert@albertgunawan.com
Claire Harwood	crharwood2000@yahoo.com
Dane Haukohl	dane.haukohl@bhpbilliton.com
Brendan Head	heabre@iinet.net.au
Craig Hilton	www.craighilton.com
Greg Hocking	www.greghocking.com
Rick Horbury	rick.horbury@csiro.au
Bo Janmaat	bo-photography@swiftdsl.com.au
Colin Kerr	yundy@tpg.com.au
Danny Khoo	www.dannykhoo.com
Stef King	www.stefking.com.au
Kingsley Klau	www.wise-klau.com.au
Greg Lewis	greg@kingbrownmag.com
Roel Loopers	www.profilephoto.com.au
Jan Lowe	janlowe@mac.com
Rick McDowell	ricphoto@iinet.net.au
Samille Mitchell	samille@wn.com.au
Misty Norman	mistynorman@bigpond.com
Kevin O'Brien	www.blackstump.biz/gallery
Richard Pappas	richard@city-life.com.au
Paul Parin	www.studioreddust.com.au
Jane Pelusey	www.pelusey.com
Michael Pelusey	www.pelusey.com
Darryl Peroni	dperoni@webace.com.au
Callum Ponton	smallpond89@hotmail.com
Derek Pool	photographics.busselton@swpp.com.au
Tobias Port	www.panoramahunter.com
Heather Reading	www.redimages.com.au
Zed Rengel	zedrengel@yahoo.com.au
Kamil Seda	kseda1@yahoo.com.au
Ivan Shaw	ivanshaw201@hotmail.com
Kathy Sheridan	followmephotos@optusnet.com.au
Hae Soo Shin	shs5@hotmail.com
Luke Simon	www.lukesimonphotography.com.au
Morland Smith	oro@iinet.net.au
Van Viet Thanh Son	vvtson@yahoo.com
Christian Sprogoe	info@csfoto.com.au
Helena Taelor	helena.taelor@central.wa.edu.au
Steinberg Tan	stguitar@bigpond.net.au
Richard Tonkin	rrtonkin@tpg.com.au
Tim van Bronswijk	tim@two8.com.au
Neil Wallace	neilpics@yahoo.com
Ross Wallace	rawallace1979@yahoo.com
Lynn Webb	www.lynnwebb.com.au
Geoff White	geoff.white@dsr.wa.gov.au
Toni Wilkinson	heytoni@bigpond.com
Vikki Wilson	v.wilson@murdoch.edu.au
Mike Wishart	wishartm@hotmail.com
Aneta Wnek	www.aneta.com.au

And with thanks to:

Coli Shipping Singapore	www.coli.com.sg
Department of Land Information	www.dli.wa.gov.au
Fremantle Football Club	www.fremantlefc.com.au
Hyundai Hopman Cup	www.hopmancup.com.au
Perth Oriels	www.wanetball.com.au
Perth Wildcats	www.wildcats.com.au
Tourism Western Australia	www.westernaustralia.com
His Majesty's Theatre	www.hismajestystheatre.com.au
West Coast Eagles Football Club	www.westcoasteagles.com.au
The UWA Perth International Arts Festival	www.perthfestival.com.au